PHOTOGRAPHY IN THE MIDDLE

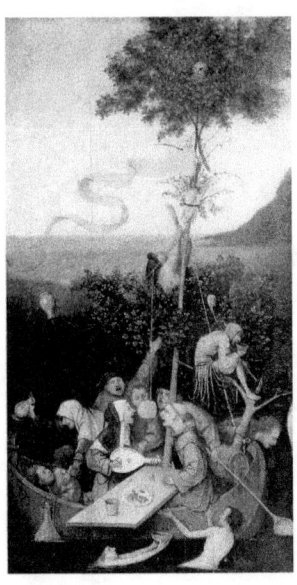

Fig. 1. Hieronymus Bosch, *Ship of Fools* (1490–1500)

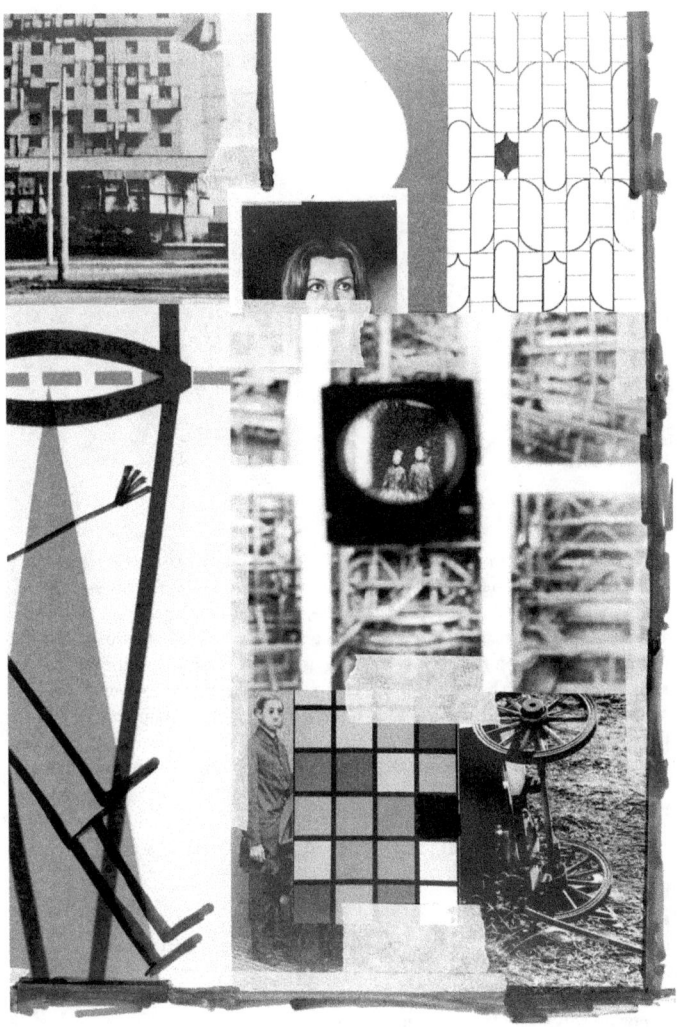

First published in 2016 by punctum books, Earth, Milky Way.
www.punctumbooks.com

ISBN-13: 978-0-9982375-1-0
ISBN-10: 0-9982375-1-5
Library of Congress Cataloging Data is available from the Library of Congress

Cover and title page design: Chris Piuma
Typography: Vincent W.J. van Gerven Oei

PHOTO-GRAPHY IN THE MIDDLE

DISPATCHES ON MEDIA ECOLOGIES AND AESTHETICS

ROB COLEY & DEAN LOCKWOOD

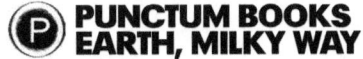 **PUNCTUM BOOKS**
EARTH, MILKY WAY

Acknowledgements

This book has taken shape over several years. Early versions of its main ideas and arguments were first presented at the following events: 'On the Verge of Photography: Imaging, Mobile Art, Humans & Computers' (Birmingham School of Art, May 2013), 'Beyond the Cut-Up: William Burroughs and the Image' (The Photographer's Gallery, London, February 2014), 'Helsinki Photomedia: Photographic Powers' (Aalto University School of Arts, Design and Architecture, March 2014), and 'Rethinking Early Photography' (University of Lincoln, June 2015). We are grateful to everyone who engaged with the ideas we presented at these events and elsewhere. Thanks especially to Adam O'Meara, with whom we have sought to experimentally explore some of these ideas in a variety of media.

Contents

List of illustrations

0 | Circle of confusion

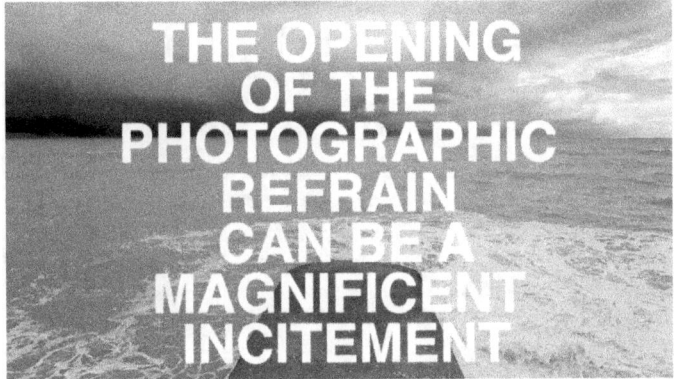

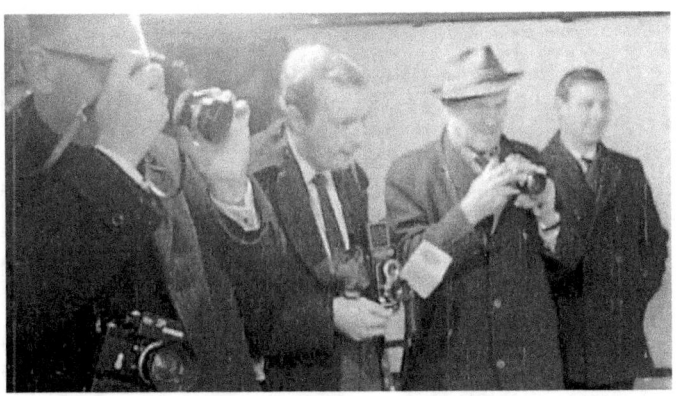

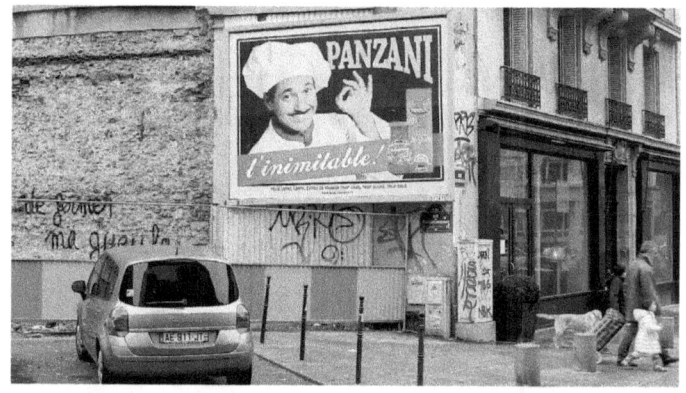

A CONSTELLATION
OF UNIVERSES
CONDUCTED
ON THE STREET,
ADJACENT
HUMAN IMAGE
EASY TO HACK

IN THE HUMANNOTHING, CUT CONDITION. TELL YOURSELF: 'NOT UNTIL WE ARE LOST...NO INTIMATE SELF TO PRESERVE'

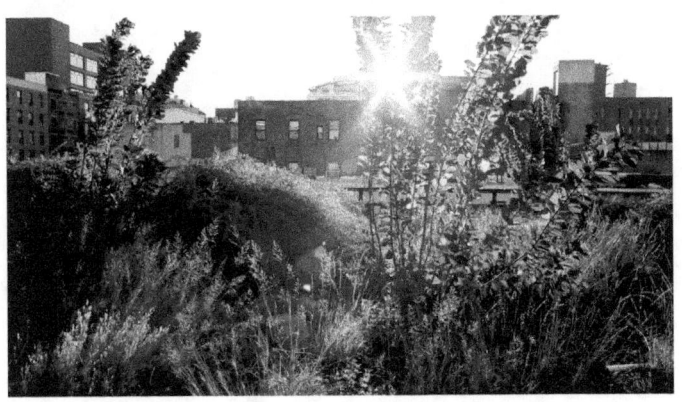

1 | Tricks learned after the crash

I knew what my old City Editor on the St Louis Post Dispatch
meant when he said: 'Go out and get that picture!'
— W.S. Burroughs

New York car accident

In the spring and summer of 1965, William Burroughs lived in a Manhattan loft apartment near Chinatown. This was a time when Burroughs was immersed in experimental media juxtaposition, cutting together written material with tape recordings and photographs, often culled from his perambulations around the streets of New York. He was in the habit of photographing traffic from above, on the iron landing of the fire escape at the front of his building.[1] One day, an accident occurred just below and Burroughs descended to capture the aftermath close up with his camera. The pictures are conspicuously undramatic, remarkably unspectacular.[2] In one, we see the crumpled hood and grill of a Chevrolet, but there is little other obvious trace of damage amongst the images. Police and passers-by stand around two or three other vehicles — including a Mack truck and a meat packers' truck — perhaps involved in the collision. There is no obvious narrative sequence. It feels like a hot day. People wear light dresses, t-shirts and shirt sleeves, peering into vehicles, pointing, smoking cigarettes,

---

1   Barry Miles, *William S. Burroughs: A Life* (London: Weidenfeld & Nicolson, 2014), 438–39.

2   The pictures, as Untitled (New York Car Accident), scanned from negatives, were exhibited at the Photographers' Gallery, London, in 2014 — twenty one images arranged in a grid of three rows, seven columns. Several of these are reproduced in the exhibition catalogue: Patricia Allmer and John Sears, *Taking Shots: The Photography of William S. Burroughs* (Munich, London & New York: Prestel Verlag, 2014), 41–48.

walking on by. Burroughs seems as much concerned to impassively plot a singular time and space as to focus on any particular object. He records the *coincidence* of bodies, vehicles, words and images. Boy-Crest clothes truck ... Kaminsky bros. safes ... a garbage basket ('Just a drop in the basket helps keep New York clean') ... a coffee shop ... jewellers ... sign for a luncheonette ... a pack of Parliament filter cigarettes on an advertising hoarding. He places himself largely at the periphery, on the sidewalk, moving behind the backs of spectators. There is nothing here approaching portraiture, little attention to faces. Burroughs occasionally moves in for a close-up of a truck's front wheel and foot board, liquid (gas?) ominously spreading out on the surface of the road from beneath the vehicle. Some pictures are shot from a distance. In one or two, there is no evidence of the accident. One, perhaps shot from his own building's fire escape, looks down upon the street — before or later? — and captures only the normal flow of traffic and activity.

Aside from ongoing media experimentation and giving a number of readings in the city, Burroughs was working flat out at the point at which these photographs were taken ('no time to breathe').[3] He was exhausted, living in fear of rumours of plans for his entrapment by the Federal Bureau of Narcotics.[4] What drove him on, it seems, was a will to complete a 'definitive' book of methods.[5] Conceived a couple of years earlier, in discussion with his collaborator, Brion Gysin, the book — with the working title, *Right Where You Are Sitting Now,* but later to be retitled, *The Third Mind* (it would not see publication for thirteen years) — appears to have preoccupied Burroughs most intensely during this period. In letters, he warns that it will be an elaborate and expensive volume, not least because of the inclusion of numerous photographic illustrations and montages. The book sets out detailed instruction in the practice of cut-ups, fold-ins, intersection pictures. It is effectively a manual, a 'how-to book', built up from the notion of an 'army bulletin' which will introduce the methods of

3   William S. Burroughs, *Rub Out the Words: Letters, 1959–1974* (London: Penguin, 2012), 195.
4   Miles, *William S. Burroughs,* 442.
5   Burroughs, *Rub Out the Words,* 190.

'the enemy' and explain how 'officers' can appropriate, frustrate and combat them.[6] Burroughs sent an extract from his early notes for the book to Gysin:

> The area in which we operate is poetry, myth, creation — The enemy can not enter this area since they are precisely non-creative and operate through machine made copies — Officers must be poets and remember that the area of poetry must be constantly reinvented. That is why cut-ups and fold-ins form one of our most vital instruments — Not only does this method recreate our area of operations but it also cuts enemy supply lines ... [7]

The enemy — 'Control' — is a semiotic machine which cues and conditions human experience, controlling reality: 'What you call "reality" is a complex network of necessity formulae ... association lines of word and image presenting a prerecorded word and image track'.[8] There is, in fact, no such thing as coincidence. Incidents are cut out from the chaos of existence, created and falling together because they have been scripted that way. 'Poetry', in the broadest sense, is the pre-constitution of a universe. Our universe is mediated in advance, pre-written and pre-photographed. Control is an 'Old Photographer', master of tricks such as the 'false click gimmick'.[9] To get the portrait you want, assemble the relevant cues, take the photograph and *then* say 'Smile!', and *then* produce a 'loud false click'. Your subject cannot prepare, cannot guard or present themselves as they wish. They do not realize they have always already been photographed, that the event of the click, in present time, is always late. Burroughs advises we pay attention — look and listen — what happens just before the click? What were you doing, thinking, feeling?[10] We live a documentary, an edited life. Victims, we are acted upon, *prone to* the present ('The first step in re-creation is to cut the old lines that hold you right

---

6   Ibid., 119.

7   Ibid.

8   William S. Burroughs and Brion Gysin, *The Third Mind* (London: John Calder, 1979), 27.

9   Ibid., 121.

10 Ibid., 5.

where you are sitting now').[11] So, how do we take 'evasive action in time', how do we dodge the bullet of the pre-photographed present? We have to assume the worst is about to happen — keep your eyes open for 'streaks' of luck, be on the look-out for conjunctions of word and image, branching together from past, through present and into the future like 'vines'.[12] Remember that incidents provoke further and similar incidents. It's a *magical* law.[13] Control neatly effaces this occult operation, but its pre-photography can be opened up and disturbed by those astute enough to be able to exploit its vulnerabilities. Poetry, art, fiction — a sorcerous practice of word and image — can locate or create ports of entry, holes or spaces in the flow of scripted and edited words and images. It can dismantle and weird destinies. *Here* is the significance of the innumerable crashes, accidents and disasters appearing in the scrapbooks and texts produced by Burroughs: symptoms of what has been called the 'hyperstitional' construction of reality.[14] The methods and techniques in *The Third Mind* are designed to liberate virtualities suppressed in the pre-constituted universe. The book is a manual for the production of a poetry of word and image, a weaponized fiction-photography to set within and against the dominant, self-effacing poetry or fiction of Control's ambitions: 'fiction acts as a Chinese Box — a container for sorcerous interventions in the world. The frame is both used (for concealment) and broken (the fictions potentiate change in reality)'.[15]

Untitled (New York Car Accident) is a vehicle, a crash or concentrate within the moment which unfurls a hyperstitional power to scan and re-constitute reality, sending out vines or tendrils into an *unknown* future. A time machine. Such experiments were explicitly conceived by Burroughs in terms of time travel. His writings and interviews during the period in question are littered with references to J.W. Dunne's reflections on the temporality of dreams (published as

11 Ibid., 28.

12 Ibid., 161.

13 Ibid., 100.

14 Cybernetic Culture Research Unit (CCRU), 'Lemurian Time War', in *Retaking the Universe: William S. Burroughs in the Age of Globalization,* ed. Davis Schneiderman and Philip Walsh (London: Pluto, 2004).

15 Ibid., 278.

An Experiment with Time, 1927).[16] For Dunne, human consciousness is fixated on a linear experience of time which enforces a relatively strict separation between past, present and future and privileges the actual and the present. However, when we dream we enter a virtuality in which everything happens at once, blended. We move more freely through time's totality which explains the precognitive phenomena often associated with dreams. Like Dunne, Burroughs recommends that we record our dreams, date them, take coordinates and look for connections, intersections between events, names, numbers, places, in the past and the future. This is not prediction of future events as such, but rather to be understood as a movement within an associational network within which our existence is entangled, more a matter of media-ecological 'possession' than subjective foresight.

Years later, Burroughs will refer to this process, after Carlos Castaneda, as a 'nagual art'.[17] Castaneda's books, which describe his initiation into the shamanic worldview of a Yaqui indian, Don Juan, distinguish between the 'tonal' universe — essentially, the predictable, pre-organized universe of Burroughs's formulation — and the magical, 'nagual' universe, unknown, unpredictable, accessed through special circumstances in which the world can be 'stopped'.[18] For Burroughs, these circumstances typically involved a random factor, an accident, perhaps a crash or the blast of a shotgun. The artist should make an ally of the accident, but no single method is guaranteed to work for ever. Gilles Deleuze and Félix Guattari shared Burroughs's interest in stopping the world through the introduction of something alien into the 'dominant atmospheric semiotic', the 'flow of interpretation, which ordinarily runs uninterruptedly'.[19] Awareness can be transformed by means of the construction of 'your own little machine' — assemble whatever elements are necessary to launch your-

---

16 See, for example, Burroughs and Gysin, *The Third Mind,* 5, 133.

17 William S. Burroughs, *Burroughs Live: The Collected Interviews of William S. Burroughs 1960–1997,* ed. Sylvère Lotringer (New York: Semiotext(e), 2001), 732.

18 Carlos Castaneda, *Journey to Ixtlan: The Lessons of Don Juan* (Harmondsworth: Penguin, 1974).

19 Gilles Deleuze and Félix Guattari, *A Thousand Plateaus* (London: Continuum, 2004), 153.

self from the 'island' of 'all that's organized and organizing' into the inhuman intensities and becomings of the nagual.[20]

For Burroughs, Control is a voice mediated and commanding through associational networks — media ecologies and aesthetics — which tame and enclose the future. It produces and organizes experiential vectors ahead of time through its command of the cut, the edit. Against this, Burroughs devotes his efforts to an 'army bulletin' in which appropriate techniques and weapons are described. His whole career, in fact, can be seen as a series of dispatches to 'officers' in the field, agents operating immanently, speculatively and experimentally from deep within the War Universe of contemporary media ecologies. The crash is a crucial figure in Burroughs's media experimentation. In and through the crash is revealed an inhuman, predatory Control Machine.

The crash is a phenomenon of time travel. To accelerate is to court the crash, and we live in times of acceleration. As Paul Virilio has argued, 'we no longer populate stationariness...we populate the *time* spent changing place, travel time'.[21] The city, for example, increasingly appears as a 'riddle' (or a 'glyph', to use Burroughs's preferred terminology), its walls and streets interrupted by hostile speeds. Where the city used to be 'located in a specific place, at the intersection of roads', now it exists 'at the intersection of practicabilities of time, in other words of speed'.[22]

War today must be of the system, the middle, taken to the immanent 'outside' from which life might be dislodged from its compromised host, the programmed human. War, as Burroughs knew, must be taken to the vectors through which Control exerts itself, a war for time-travellers, waged at the intersections. For Burroughs, as we have said, reality is a self-effacing informational edit or montage. It has to be attacked at the points at which its cover slips. It is in terms of this form of attack — exploiting deviations from the edit, rips within the 'Reality Film', as Burroughs has it — that Burroughs's photography must be understood as *war photography*.

---

20   Ibid., 179.
21   Paul Virilio and Sylvère Lotringer, *Pure War* (New York: Semiotext(e), 1983), 60.
22   Ibid., 65.

Vectors are a matter of relations rather than identities and forms. McKenzie Wark, after Virilio, suggests that information moves at such speed today that Control finds its new terrain in an abstract communicational space-time, a 'third nature' that emerges with the enclosure of both first nature and the second nature of built forms by a media and communications layer.[23] With vectoral technologies, the world is no longer framed in 'static pictures ... singular texts' but rather edited into a 'singular rhythm of cuts and ruptures', a 'continuous feed'. We now populate a space-time of information flows abstracted from territorial boundaries and the boundaries of subjects and objects. This, leaning on Deleuze and Guattari, is 'the future of the rhizome made concrete: where every trajectory is potentially connected to every other trajectory'.[24]

If we are to engage in war with the vector, Wark's assertion that the forms of our 'communicational interventions' need to be rethought in terms of the practicabilities of time, of the informational edit, has a direct bearing on how we should understand Burroughs's relevance in relation to photographic practice. The vector is beyond human command. It is a chaotic space, a mediatic space of possibility for weird, irruptive events which have to be mediated, stabilized, edited, reined in by dominant refrains and narratives at the same time as there is that about them which remains beyond mediation.[25] Wark suggests that such events are crucial because they illuminate, like the 'after-image' left by a lightning flash, the shape of the vector, the very possibility space giving rise to the event.[26] We will note, later, how Burroughs and Gysin ventured to contact and question Control, with some limited success dependent upon a temporary set of arrangements.[27] If Control answers us today, however, it answers only as it betrays itself through weird events occurring within, and briefly illuminating, the aforementioned possibility space.

---

23 McKenzie Wark, *Telesthesia: Communication, Culture and Class* (Cambridge: Polity, 2012).

24 Ibid., 35.

25 Ibid., 64.

26 Ibid., 68.

27 See Brion Gysin, *Here to Go: Planet R-101 — Brion Gysin interviewed by Terry Wilson* (London: Quartet Books, 1985), 215–32.

Hit and run

New York City again. 1927, the early days of the war. It's a surreal story, totally surreal. You've heard it before but it goes something like this: Lee Miller, 19 years old, sets out from her rented brownstone apartment — one of those nice places up on West 48th Street — and joins the crowd hurrying about on the street below. Only, she's not really looking where she's going, and steps off the sidewalk right into the traffic, right in front of an oncoming car. As it bears down on her (imagine it in slow motion if it helps) the driver of the car is yelling, honking his horn, other drivers doing the same, when suddenly, out of nowhere, and just at the last second, someone pulls her back to safety. Phew. This girl Miller, who's only been back in the US a while after spending almost a year in Paris, is so shocked that she starts gabbling away in French to her rescuer. Best of all, it turns out that this regular one-in-a-million New York hero is none other than Condé Montrose Nast, the publishing magnate. Now, Nast has a bit of an eye for the ladies, if you know what I mean, but he's *really* struck by Miller — that slender figure, that androgynous hairstyle, that chic French outfit — this is a girl who embodies the tempo of the age, he thinks. This is the girl he's been looking for. So, right then and there, he signs her up as a model for Vogue, and within a few short months she's on the cover.[28]

Miller's crash exists only in the virtual. A concertinaed present throws out multiple future trajectories. In the familiar story, this one incident, this chance encounter, catapults Miller into a whole series of future events: in Nast's Park Avenue penthouse she picks up photography from Edward Steichen; in Paris she hangs out with the likes of Man Ray, Jean Cocteau, André Breton, Paul Éluard, Max Ernst and Pablo Picasso; in New York she runs a photographic studio popular with the glitterati; in Cairo she plans and conducts complex expedi-

---

28 Versions of this story are recounted in most texts on Miller. See, for example: Carolyn Burke, *Lee Miller: A Life* (Chicago: University of Chicago Press, 2007), 56; Becky E. Conekin, *Lee Miller in Fashion* (London: Thames and Hudson, 2013), 22; Becky E. Conekin, 'Lee Miller's Simultaneity: Photographer and Model in the Pages of Inter-war Vogue,' in *Fashion as Photograph: Viewing and Reviewing Images of Fashion*, ed. Eugenie Shinkle (London: I.B. Tauris, 2008) 73; Anthony Penrose, *The Lives of Lee Miller* (London: Thames and Hudson, 2013), 16.

tions into the Egypt desert; in Saint Malo, as a respected photojournalist, she digs in with the 83rd Infantry Division of the US Army; in Dachau she's one of the first to enter the concentration camp after liberation, and in Munich, later that same day, she takes a bath at Hitler's house. So many lives in one life. So surreal, right? No, not quite. Agent Miller knows better.

In case we forget, the surreal is not simply a synonym for something peculiar, something odd. André Breton would have something to say about that. For him, like Burroughs, the human sensorium offers defective access to the world. In Breton's account, our everyday habits of thinking and perceiving are too narrowly confined to conscious reality, whereas surreality is an 'absolute reality' recovered in the dialectical resolution of contradictory states: internal and external worlds, unconscious dreams and conscious reality.[29] Without any of the critical horror that marks out Burroughs and Gysin from the surrealists, Breton reveled in chance encounters and coincidence on the basis that the bizarre and seemingly incompatible juxtapositions produced in such encounters recuperate the lost psychic powers of the unconscious. They restore to the modern individual untimely connections that allow the world to be experienced in a different way.[30] The invisible is rendered visible. Breton demanded that we 'not lose sight of the fact that the idea of Surrealism aims quite simply at the total recovery of our psychic force by a means which is nothing other than the dizzying descent into ourselves, the systematic illumination of hidden places and the progressive darkening of other places...'[31]

Amidst all this, there tend to be two versions of Lee Miller's story. There is the story that confirms her credentials as surrealist artist in her own right, and not simply as muse and lover, not simply dirigible lips and metronomic eye. Then there is the story of a photographer whose advertising and documentary work is inspired by Surrealism but whose role within the movement itself amounts to that of con-

29 André Breton, 'Manifesto of Surrealism', in *Manifestoes of Surrealism* (Ann Arbor: University of Michigan Press, 1972 [1924]), 14.

30 Ibid., 45.

31 André Breton, 'Second Manifesto of Surrealism', in *Manifestoes of Surrealism* (Ann Arbor: University of Michigan Press, 1972 [1930]), 136–37.

servator, a chronicler of great men. Both take the form of fantastical Bildungsroman — a story we have heard before. In Miller's case, though, the story is camouflage, a trick, a stratagem. Hers is not a surreal story.

Surrealism, which according to Breton could just as easily be called supernaturalism, in fact sought to domesticate real weirdness, to render it human, to reduce it to questions of the unconscious, to a reality that has been repressed but can be awakened.[32] Where Burroughs is possessed, surrealism possesses. Where Burroughs glimpses a hostile entity, surrealism unleashes ostensibly emancipatory forces. Yet the surrealist's principal media technique of psychic automatism 'led to no new perspective', and was swiftly replaced by artist strategies that were 'individual and deliberate'.[33] Such strategies suggest a retreat. Perhaps the surrealists had glimpsed something terrifying. At best, surreality is a tame weirdness, where the desire to liberate thought and perception, inspired by esoteric mysticism, is inhibited and constrained by a simultaneous desire to formalize and regulate such energies.[34]

In the roaring twenties, the desire to augment and enhance human subjectivity was expressed in various ways. For example, in 1927, a few months after Miller's non-crash, and a couple of years before The Big Crash, the now celebrated Machine-Age Exposition was staged in a bare New York loft space. Alongside Man Ray's rayographs, the event celebrated the construction of second nature (photographs of electrical plants, factories and warehouses, which sat alongside drawings of motor cars, models of aeroplanes, and machine guns), and showcased the infrastructure of an incipient third nature (photographs of broadcasting stations, set alongside radio sets). Curated by Jane Heap of The Little Review, the show was concerned with a certain kind of technologically mediated vitality, the much-discussed 'tempo of the age' that was transforming and accel-

---

32 Breton, 'Manifesto of Surrealism', 25.
33 '23 Stitches Taken by Gerard-Georges Lemair and 2 Points of Order by Brion Gysin' in Burroughs and Gysin, The Third Mind, 12.
34 For an account of the links between Surrealism and the occult, see Patrick Lepetit, Esoteric Secrets of Surrealism: Origins, Magic, and Secret Societies (Rochester, VT: Inner Traditions, 2014).

erating human relations with technology.[35] Charles Lindbergh's flight over the Atlantic Ocean, completed at the time of the exposition, seemed to explicitly demonstrate such processes, though Heap was most directly inspired by the teachings of spiritualist G.I. Gurdjieff (whose life was punctuated by two near-fatal car accidents). In the exposition catalogue, Heap declares that the selected art works are 'organizing and transforming the realities of our age into a dynamic beauty', which is to say they are the works of artists who do not simply imitate or worship the machine but 'recognize it as one of the realities'.[36] Here, the increasing tempo of relations between human and nonhuman machine is understood to provoke a state of transcendence, technomystical enlightenment, machine-being.

For his part, Breton does at least come to acknowledge that the human may not be at the centre of all things. There may be other forms of agency in the world, he later muses, nonhuman 'creatures' invisible to human habits of perception: 'Nothing necessarily stands in the way of these creatures being able to completely escape man's sensory system of references through a camouflage of whatever sort one cares to imagine'.[37] But ultimately, he remains caught in the paradox where any attempt to conceive the world-in-itself, 'a world in some inaccessible, already given state', becomes the world-for-us, 'the world that we, as human beings, interpret and give meaning to'.[38] Nonhuman vectors are anthropomorphized.

Though Miller escaped unscathed, that near miss on West 48th Street dislodged ontological and epistemological coordinates that were previously fixed. Her story, as it is usually recounted, is a tale of 'many lives', a story in which Miller continually reinvents herself, in front of and behind the camera, moving through different worlds, responding to people, places and events. We might, though, read

---

35 See Susan Noyes Platt, 'Mysticism in the Machine Age: Jane Heap and The Little Review', *Twenty One/Art and Culture* 1.1 (1989): 34.

36 Jane Heap, *Machine-Age Exposition Catalogue* (New York: 119 West 57th Street, 1927), 36.

37 André Breton, 'Prolegomena to a Third Surrealist Manifesto or Not', in *Manifestoes of Surrealism* (Ann Arbor: University of Michigan Press, 1972 [1942]), 293.

38 Eugene Thacker, *In the Dust of This Planet: Horror of Philosophy Vol. 1* (Winchester and Washington: Zero Books, 2011), 4.

her story as one of mediation, a story of ruptured and entangled subjectivity where humans and media technologies are inseparably joined, part of the same process. We might recognize it as a story that confirms we are media, that we are physically and ontologically bound up with the technological environment: 'As we modify and extend "our" technologies and "our" media, we modify and extend ourselves and our environments'.[39] Technology is the force of mediation that brings forth the world, the force through which we become with the world. We are in a process of coemergence with technology, always already in relation to it, always already, in a sense, outside ourselves. The nonhuman is the condition of possibility and condition of *im*possibility of the human. We evolve creatively, we are made and unmade technologically, technopoietically, and we ought not to conceive of ourselves as autonomous controllers of such a process of creative evolution. Accordingly, a story of mediation demands that we scrutinize more closely the very notion of mediation. In their recent attempt to do just this, Alexander Galloway, Eugene Thacker and McKenzie Wark begin by problematizing the tendency, in media and cultural theory, to presume successful communication. They focus instead on the 'insufficiency of mediation', noting that 'every communication harbours the dim awareness of an excommunication that is prior to it, that conditions it and makes it all the more natural.'[40] Theirs is a 'theory of mediation as excommunication', a theory adequate to thinking the worlding processes of media beyond the human.

Miller, we might say, developed her own sensibility to such processes, and to their instabilities. Rather than offering a privileged position, this sensibility comes from an understanding that it is impossible to separate oneself out from one's various relations, particularly as these relations become ever more intense. Perhaps, in this story, the virtual trajectories of Miller's non-crash become actualized elsewhere: excommunicated in the air crash experienced by her lover,

---

39 Sarah Kember and Joanna Zylinska, *Life After New Media: Mediation as a Vital Process* (Cambridge, MA: MIT Press, 2012), 13.

40 Alexander Galloway, Eugene Thacker, and McKenzie Wark, 'Execrable Media', in *Excommunication: Three Inquiries in Media and Mediation* (Chicago and London: University of Chicago Press: 2014), 10.

Argylle, shortly after buzzing the ship that carried Miller from New York to Paris, or in her visit to an Egyptian village where, 'unfortunately I ran over a man or something…if you hit anyone out here in the country, you are expected to beat it — in fact the Consulates always say HIT AND RUN'.[41] Hit and run, for Miller, is a trick, a stratagem for life in an ever more intensely mediated world. Her story is surreal only insofar that surrealism points to the way that processes of mediation work, enables a practical exploration of how things operate, and hints at what media *does*. This practical exploration means taking a hit, or in Burroughs's terms being pre-photographed, which is to say, being unconsciously activated, primed toward certain behaviour. Crashes, accidents in the darkroom, etc., allow brief glimpses at these programmed affordances — as Burroughs put it, '[a]ll photographers will tell you that often their best shots are accidents' — but nothing systematic can be learned from or developed in response to such occurrences.[42] They remain, at best, the material of 'operative constructs', and must be experimented with in the context of different practices, used in relation to different techniques and technologies.[43] More seriously, 'the pragmatics of a stratagem always risk misfiring', the effects of crashes are real, even if they are not yet actual.[44] Sometimes you just have to run. Burroughs: 'old photographer tricks and tricks don't always work. (My jujitsu instructor used to say: "If your trick no work, you better run.")'[45]

Into the ditch

Around mid-day on the 15th October 1908, as reported in the local *Evening Courier*, F.T. Marinetti, driving along the Via Domodossola in the industrialized outskirts of Milan, swerved to avoid a cy-

---

41 As she sailed away from New York to Paris in 1929, the year of The Great Crash, her lover, Argylle, piloted his biplane so close to the sundeck of the ship that he could release a flurry of roses to mark her departure. The aviator crashed the aircraft later that same day (Burke, *Lee Miller*, 383). For Miller's letter to her brother in which she obliquely notes the car accident, see Penrose, *The Lives of Lee Miller*, 65.

42 Burroughs and Gysin, *The Third Mind*, 29.

43 Matthew Fuller and Andrew Goffey, *Evil Media* (Cambridge, MA: MIT Press, 2012), 21.

44 Ibid., 22.

45 Burroughs and Gysin, *The Third Mind*, 28.

clist and overturned his vehicle in the ditch running alongside the road.[46] Two other drivers (apparently from the factory from which Marinetti's car had been very recently produced) stopped to assist. Neither Marinetti nor his passenger, a mechanic friend, was seriously injured but the car was severely battered. Marinetti would have attracted attention with this expensive acquisition. Few could aspire to the purchase of a four-cylinder Fiat Isotta Fraschini 'Gran Lusso' (Grand Luxury). In a photo, taken before the accident, he sits proudly at the wheel, the car in profile. After the accident, photos capture a bemused crowd gathered to inspect the wreckage at the bottom of the ditch, curious children crouching on the muddy bank for the best view. In his fictionalized retelling of the event, installed as a convenient origin story at the beginning of his 'Foundation and Manifesto of Futurism', published widely in Italy and beyond in 1909, Marinetti describes the slow extraction of car from ditch, in the process of which bodywork and upholstery were shed. Miraculously, he reports, the frame of this 'great shark that had been washed up and stranded' remained in working order.[47] Together with this harder, leaner, lighter monster, Marinetti had been reborn ('O mother of a ditch, brimful with muddy water!'), ready to accelerate from the crash site with a new aesthetic, a new poetics of speed and cult of the machine.

In the introduction to the manifesto, we are told how Marinetti and his 'lads', after a long night of debate, 'trailing out age-old indolence back and forth over richly adorned, oriental carpets', were roused, at dawn, by the racket of vehicles in the street, to leap into their own 'panting beasts' and to tear insanely towards the violent conception of their movement in the muddy ditch.[48] The manifesto extols the virtues of the racing car, famously rendered, by its speed

---

46 Cited in Christine Poggi, *Inventing Futurism: The Art and Politics of Artificial Optimism* (Princeton: Princeton University Press, 2009), 7.

47 Filippo Tommaso Marinetti, 'The Foundation and Manifesto of Futurism', in *Critical Writings*, ed. Gunter Berghaus (New York: Farrar, Straus and Giroux), 13.

48 Marinetti, 'The Foundation and Manifesto of Futurism', 11, 12. Berghaus comments, in a footnote (427–28) that his salon was 'filled with Oriental clutter, which had been brought back from Alexandria in Egypt, where his family had lived for thirty years'.

and noise, 'more beautiful than the Winged Victory of Samothrace'.[49] This is reckless life, 'life at the double'.[50] The art and poetry proper to it 'must be thought of as a violent assault upon the forces of the unknown with the intention of making them prostrate themselves at the feet of mankind'.[51]

According to Christine Poggi, Marinetti later circulated the idea that the crash occurred on the 11th October, rather than the 15th, 'because eleven was a significant number for him. There were eleven points in the first Futurist manifesto, and most manifestos were dated the eleventh of the month'.[52] Everything revolved around the explosive, accelerant potential of the manifesto as form. This famous crash which marked the birth of a certain brand of modernist radicalism writ large the claim for the ascendance of a new order of reality from the ashes of the old, an order of speed. Just as, it seems, cars and cyclists cannot reasonably coexist amongst the velocities of the modern city, and just as the indolence of the bourgeois interior cannot survive the bracing winds of technological progress, so new — *faster, sharper* — literary and poetic forms would arise which would be incommensurate with the sluggish and turbid rhythms of tradition.

In 1911, Marinetti was employed as a war correspondent in Libya, covering the Italo-Turkish war for a Paris newspaper. His experiences of battle cried out for a novel use of language, a poetry tantamount to combat which would be capable of an invigorating communication of the violence of modern life by its very material embodiment.[53] Put simply, thrown into an experience of great intensity by war or disaster, one learns to communicate quickly, briefly, forcefully. One communicates strictly what is required and does away with niceties. Although Marinetti conceded that journalists, politicians, philosophers and so forth were bound to make sense to their readers by recourse to syntax and punctuation, the poet should know no

---

49 Marinetti, 'The Foundation and Manifesto of Futurism', 13.

50 Ibid.

51 Ibid.

52 Poggi, *Inventing Futurism*, 274.

53 John J. White, 'Iconic and indexical elements in Italian Futurist poetry: F.T. Marinetti's 'words-in-freedom'', in *Signergy*, ed. C. Jac Conradie et al. (Amsterdam and Philadelphia: John Benjamins Publishing, 2010), 137.

such constraint and, in fact, is duty bound to liberate words, to get to the heart of the matter. The poet 'will thus convey life's analogical bedrock, telegraphically, that is, with the same economical rapidity that the telegraph imposes on reporters and war correspondents in their summary reports'.[54] Sensibilities are shifted dramatically by new forms of media and transportation, notably with respect to speed and rhythm. The poet must respond, celebrating 'multiple and simultaneous consciousnesses in the same individual'.[55] The poet must 'make connections between things that have no apparent connection, *without using conductor wires,* but rather condensed *Words-in-Freedom*'.[56] In this situation, poetry, he decreed, 'must be a continuous stream of new images' — only the orchestration of a 'tight network' of words and images can 'gather together all that which is most fleeting and elusive in materiality'.[57] Such a poetry shrugs off the yoke of psychologism and anthropomorphism. It sets out through, for example, the dismantling of syntax and of individual words, the refusal of punctuation, of adjectives and adverbs, the liberal application of startling onomatopoeia, typographical experimentation, to body forth inhuman 'molecular life':[58]

> take care not to bestow human feelings on matter; guess rather what its different determining impulses will be, its compressive and its expansive forces, what binds it, what breaks it down, its mass of swarming molecules or its swirling electrons.[59]

Marinetti's rebirth in the muddy matrix of the ditch, coupled with his insistence on cultivating a vibrant form of expression immanent to, resonant with, 'molecular life', seems, at first glance, to speak to contemporary approaches in 'new materialism' such as Jane Ben-

---

54 Marinetti, 'Destruction of Syntax-Untrammeled Imagination-Words-in-Freedom', in *Critical Writings*, 123.

55 Ibid., 121.

56 Ibid., 123.

57 Marinetti, 'Technical Manifesto of Futurist Literature', in *Critical Writings*, 109.

58 Marinetti, 'Destruction of Syntax-Untrammeled Imagination-Words-in-Freedom', 125.

59 Marinetti, 'Technical Manifesto of Futurist Literature', 111.

nett's theorization of the non-human agency of a 'vital materiality'.[60] However, Marinetti was committed to a modernist radicalism which had ruptured with the past, comprising an embrace of technology such that human limitations could be overcome. 'We are not joking,' he will write in 1910, 'when we declare that in human flesh wings lie dormant'.[61] Marinetti attempts to speed the advent of the 'day when it will be possible for man to externalize his will so that, like a huge invisible arm, it can extend beyond him, then his Dream and his Desire, which today are merely idle words, will rule supreme over conquered Space and Time'.[62] Against this commitment to a radical break and an ultimate conquest, we would rather commend a view beginning with unmitigated entanglement of the human with the 'catastrophe' that is matter, with inhuman media ecologies. In the twenty-first century, human experience is entangled with media networks which increasingly operate beneath conscious perceptual awareness. As Mark Hansen argues, agent-centred perceptual consciousness cedes to a pervasive environmental sensibility.[63] In contemporary media ecologies we are compelled to come to terms with our pre-personal embeddedness and continuity with the world.

This sensibility is to be found in Tom McCarthy's re-staging of Marinetti's crash in his novel, C. The novel's protagonist, Serge Carrefax, ensnared in oppressive circumstances, 'decides he's got to make things move' and races out of London fast enough that he can 're-find the stasis in the motion'.[64] It is as if he has penetrated a 'projected image' which in turn penetrates him.[65] The air, the space, the colours through which he passes 'become material' and, when he flips his car over into a ditch and is immured inside the vehicle — 'my own crypt' — the very dirt penetrates him, earth inside his mouth.[66]

60 Jane Bennett, *Vibrant Matter: A Political Ecology of Things* (Durham and London: Duke University Press, 2010).

61 Marinetti, 'Extended Man and the Kingdom of the Machine', in *Critical Writings*, 86.

62 Ibid.

63 Mark B.N. Hansen, *Feed-Forward: On the Future of Twenty-First Century Media* (Chicago and London: University of Chicago Press, 2015).

64 Tom McCarthy, *C* (London: Jonathan Cape, 2010), 235.

65 Ibid.

66 Ibid., 236.

Waking in hospital, he embraces this passive immersivity as if a willing 'minor character' in an endless film.[67] To go into the image (into the 'Reality Film', as Burroughs puts it) is to become spectral, networked, immanent to the materiality of media ecologies. McCarthy's hermetic re-staging of Marinetti's origin myth places the emphasis on descent, entanglement and encryption rather than birth. Marinetti does stress dirt and materiality — he rises from his ditch foul, stinking — but where he is singled out and lent strength by the sludgy encounter, launched into a heroic future, for McCarthy, the 'real disaster' is the insignificance of our disaster.[68] As Nieland comments, 'progressive medial inevitabilities are revealed to be techno-fantasies. All that is inevitable in the novel is entropic movement into the earth, the subterranean, the burrow, the underworld... what Serge, near the novel's end, calls the "real disaster", which is just the loss of human "catastrophe" itself — its "rubbing out" in inhuman, geological time'.[69]

The life of McCarthy's early twentieth-century protagonist is the pretext for an archaeology of media in which the human is fatally entangled with the catastrophe that is matter. Burroughs's New York car accident was bound up with a conception of the camera as a scrambling device which expresses the power of time travel, the attunement of the present to zones of futurity — a 'paraphotographic' (as we will say) synchronicity through which typical patterns of recognition are processed intro transformative encounters (or, in Burroughs's terminology, 'intersection pictures'). McCarthy conceives photography in somewhat similar terms, suggesting that

> to talk about the medium's past or future, or those of the world, makes no sense, since these categories belong to the linear timescale of Enlightenment. But we're talking endarkenment here; unshaped plasma in which pixels drift, collide and separate in prehistoric or pre-figurative frenzy; noxious fluid mulch where pasts,

---

67 Ibid., 237.
68 Ibid., 278.
69 Justus Nieland, 'Dirty Media: Tom McCarthy and the Afterlife of Modernism', *Modern Fiction Studies* 58.3 (2012): 594.

futures and presents, all composted, lurk as potentiality and immanence — that is, as fiction.[70]

This predilection for encryption and obscurity — photography as a negativity and dark virtuality redolent of weird fiction (and there will be more to say about fabulation and the weird as we go along) — is of a piece with McCarthy's reflexive explorations, in his fiction and with his comrades in the International Necronautical Society (INS), of the form and function of the avant-garde manifesto and artistic communication and the aesthetics of transmission and mediation more broadly.[71] Carrefax's crash spurns the form and force of Marinetti's manifesto. It completely undercuts its urgency in failing to rush to the new, the next.[72] In fact, in the wake of the crash, Carrefax reverses Marinetti's direction of flight and, where Marinetti and his family moved from Egypt to Europe, Carrefax travels from Europe to Egypt to work for the British army on a 'theory of telegraphic immortality' and to become embroiled in an archaeological dig.[73] Just as, with his work for the INS, it is death rather than the Future which is the abiding concern, so here, 'McCarthy suggests the manifesto's impossibility, the impossibility of change, new, and now'.[74]

However, perhaps there is still something in the manifesto, something that can be squeezed from its brevity, its speed. Perhaps this is better thought through the dispatch, the 'summary report' or the how-to manual for officers in the field. Even though the 'lazy meme' of the Future must surely be interrogated in the light of the insight that the new, like the now, is 'always already mediated', always pre-photographed, there is, again with Burroughs, something that we

---

70 Tom McCarthy, 'Science & Fiction, with a text by Tom McCarthy', *The Photographers' Gallery Blog*, 15 June 2014, http://thephotographersgalleryblog.org. uk/2014/06/15/science-and-fiction-with-a-text-by-tom-mccarthy.

71 See Tom McCarthy, Simon Critchley et al., *The Mattering of Matter: Documents from the Archive of the International Necronautical Society* (Berlin: Sternberg Press, 2012).

72 Laura McGrath, 'McCarthy, Marinetti and the Manifesto: New, Now and Never', *Emerging Modernisms*, 17 August 2012, https://emergingmodernisms.wordpress. com/2012/08/17/mccarthy-marinetti-and-the-manifesto-new-now-and-never.

73 Ibid.

74 Ibid.

might 'feel our way toward: the breach, the sudden, epiphanic emergence of the unplanned, the departure from the script'.[75] The crash, the disaster, the catastrophe, is a crucial figure for the contemporary age and its media ecologies. It is, we believe, intimately bound up with the flash and cut of photography. However, the crash is temporally strange — weird. It is of the Endarkenment's version of time rather than the Enlightenment's version; backwards and immanent, failing to progress, proper to 'entrenchment' rather than unobstructed flight.[76] In Burroughs's War Universe, the properly endarkened form of communication might be, we hazard, the dispatch. A different kind of molecularity of word and image to the networks imagined by Marinetti, the risky dispatch from the lost, dark middle which reeks of crisis, disappointment, resignation and abandonment — is anyone receiving? — might itself be constitutive of, as McCarthy says, channelling Burroughs, 'a new catastrophe to counter the ongoing one'.[77] A critical horror, perhaps.

Nova crash

So far the crash has triggered encounters with manifestos of method, communiqués on that which is desirable to communicate, on that which *can* be communicated. Crashes and non-crashes have invoked movement, they have aroused progress, they have activated radical breaks, rebirths. Now, though, we find ourselves in a situation where communication is silenced. The crash resigns us to defeat, to our doom.

Defeat: Suffering various ailments — duodenal ulcer, hernia, the effects of a heart attack — and, at the age of sixty-six, routed at the Eastern Front, Marinetti retreats to Lake Como. There, at dawn, in the Hotel Splendido, he succumbs to a second heart attack. Mussolini affords him a state funeral, but as Il Duce's Fascist state turns against its own people Fascism is collapsing too.[78]

---

75 McCarthy, Critchley et al., *The Mattering of Matter*, 267, 276.

76 Ibid., 269–70.

77 Ibid., 273.

78 Ernest Ialongo, *Filippo Tommaso Marinetti: The Artist and His Politics* (Fairleigh Dickinson University Press, 2015), 296–98.

Resignation: In the aftermath of the end of the Second World War, Miller spends a year moving around Eastern Europe, searching in vain for new coordinates, stimulation. Eventually, skin drained of colour, blistered lips, bleeding gums, she begrudgingly returns to England and marries the 'friendly surrealist' Ronald Penrose. The rest of her life unfolds in a fug of whisky and Benzedrine, self-loathing and misery. She retreats into cookery, rarely taking photographs.

Doomed: In his latter years, holed up in Kansas, Burroughs all but gives up writing to focus instead on painting. The cut-up ultimately proves a dead end, it fails to overcome the forces it is targeted against, forces that will inevitably destroy the planet.

One of the collages included in *The Third Mind* assembles two existing cut-ups, both of which compose material in relation to a fragment of printed text: 'NOVA EXPRESS'. This is, of course, the title of Burroughs's experimental novel, published the year previously, in which he confronts the visceral forces of Control as rendered in the guise of the Nova Mob. Both of the media collages mimic a newspaper layout. In the first, the bold text 'NOVA EXPRESS' appears beneath a photograph of a train crash, an image that is itself placed beneath words that identify this fictional section of a newspaper as one that records disasters and crimes. A column of Burroughs's own typewritten text runs along the left side of the collage and announces, 'you are reading the future…'

It may be tempting to interpret this collage as a comment on the train wreck of historical progress, as a Burroughsian counterpart to Paul Klee's *Angelus Novus*, an image famously described by Walter Benjamin as depicting the 'angel of history' surveying the wreckage of the past as it is propelled backwards into the future.[79] Indeed, Burroughs articulates an explicit concern for humanity's accelerated trajectory toward planetary catastrophe. The novel *Nova Express* opens with 'last words', words from a planet on which forces of control have moved 'to sell out the unborn'.[80] As he put it, these last words 'are not

---

79 Walter Benjamin, *Selected Writings, vol. 4, 1938–1940,* ed. Howard Eiland and Michael W. Jennings (Cambridge, MA: Harvard University Press, 2003), 392.

80 William S. Burroughs, *Nova Express: The Restored Text,* ed. Oliver Harris (New York: Grove Press, 2014 [1964]), 4.

premature. These words may be too late.'[81] The Nova Mob operates through vectors of control that manipulate and provoke anthropogenic destruction. All of his work, Burroughs says elsewhere, is directed against forces 'bent, though stupidity or design, on blowing up the planet or rendering it uninhabitable.'[82] In this sense it might also be tempting to conceive derailment as the result of revolution, with Burroughs's experiments contributing to what Benjamin called 'an attempt by passengers on the train — namely, the human race — to activate the emergency brake.'[83]

Yet, as Oliver Harris argues, the tendency to scrutinize the content or message of this collage (the tendency to be preoccupied with the train) overlooks the importance of its form or medium.[84] In Harris's account, there is something specific about Burroughs's concern with speed, and this is revealed in the second of the two collages. Here, the word 'EXPRESS' is deliberately cut from the banner of British newspaper the *Daily Express*, a consequence of Burroughs's obsession with the communicational trajectories of third nature. For him, 'NOVA' designates the new(s), the speed of communication, the processes of technological abstraction that, nonetheless, have utterly material consequences. Third nature is inscribed in — and inseparable from — both first and second nature. Third nature inhabits and pierces the body. Here lies the real motivation of Burroughs's 'last words' — to invoke a heretical mode of communication targeted at its own negation. Rather than seeking to apply an emergency brake, Burroughs summons a different kind of *break*, a departure from what Galloway, Thacker and Wark call 'the community of believers', an excommunication that does not mean exile from the conventional system of communication, even though it means he is incapable of participating in its established rituals.[85] Expelled by circumstance from such communication, Burroughs's 'intermediary status', his middleness, allows him to conduct experiments with the processes

81   Ibid.
82   Cited in Miles, *William S Burroughs,* 429.
83   Benjamin, *Selected Writings,* 4:402.
84   Oliver Harris, 'The Future Leaks Out', in William S. Burroughs, *Nova Express: The Restored Text* (New York: Grove Press, 2014).
85   Galloway, Thacker and Wark, 'Execrable Media', 15.

and procedures through which history is made, and the future trajectories with which we are integrated.[86]

This is because, for him, Nova is nothing new. Though Control effects an alien invasion of the human, it is an ancient force, an originary inhuman vector of the human, humanity's originary endarkenment. In *The Beginning Is Also The End*, a short text written in 1963, Burroughs presents an interview with Mr Martin, The Man of A Thousand Lies, the leader of the Nova Mob and representative of an alien power that requires human hosts for its survival.[87] Mr Martin recounts how he was brought to earth by accident, in a crash, half a million years ago: 'My arrival here was a wreck. The ship came apart like a rotten undervest.'[88] Control as an ancient alien, present for so long it has become invisible. Here the question of control is at the centre of what it is to be human. To be human is to be infected with the word and image virus of control — to be parasited and to be a parasite. We are media. The human is a site of inhuman mediation. As Mr Martin makes clear, the ancient invasion of the human takes place by means of seeding a 'prerecorded film' in the human body, 'virus negatives' that await development in the human darkroom. It is, Mr Martin says, 'a simple operation', one that does not impose power on human activity but mediates the conditions within which such activity emerges, meaning that such activity is encouraged to unfold in ways that seem natural, aesthetic. As Mr Martin delights in telling us, this means that humans 'cannot think or conceive in non-image terms' precisely because any process of thought is pre-photographed, as he puts it, a product of 'my biologic film which is a series of images.' Any attempt to conceive the world-in-itself is reduced to a world-for-us. The natural state of the human is one based on addic-

---

86 On an 'intermediary status' see ibid., 15. For a response to the anti-accelerationist demand for an emergency brake, see McKenzie Wark 'The Drone of Minerva', Public Seminar, 5 November 2014. http://www.publicseminar.org/2014/11/the-drone-of-minerva/#.Vci-1UWVJpl.

87 Inspector Lee describes Mr Martin as the leader of the nova mob in *The Ticket That Exploded* (William S. Burroughs (London: Fourth Estate, 2010 [1962]).

88 William S. Burroughs, 'The Beginning is Also the End', in *The Burroughs File* (San Francisco: City Lights, 1984), 62–66. All quotations in the paragraph are from this source.

tion — once a single virus negative has been developed an aesthetic pattern is established, human activities become 'drearily predictable', they conform to a programme: 'It should now be obvious that what you call "reality" is a function of these precisely predictable because prerecorded human activities.'

Yet this addiction occurs in both directions. The entity 'Mr Martin' is so named for the sake of communication. It has no self beyond the human hosts to which it is addicted: 'I am reality and I am hooked, on, reality.' Blinded in the crash that brought him to earth, Mr Martin has cultivated human culture as a device through which to explore the possibility of escape. Human culture is a probe-head, the negative nerve endings of Control, a means for exploring possible trajectories: 'What you call the history of mankind is the history of my escape plan.' On occasion this arrangement threatens the stability of control, there are ruptures in the aesthetic, non-natural breaches in nature. Certain individuals — Rimbaud, Tzara, numerous others whose names we will never know — 'got too close one way or another'. But as Mr Martin makes clear, he has 'ways of dealing with wise guys… Tricks I learned after the crash.' The Nova crash begets the generative power of the negative.[89] The zone of the accident, and every accident that follows, is momentarily charged with indeterminacy, an absence that teems with present potential, a force that can be carefully mediated. Movement along particular trajectories is encouraged, aestheticized, while movement along others is inhibited, made to perish. The virus of mutual addiction maintains a state of dynamic stability.

The force of the negative dominates that most mythologized episode of Burroughs's life — the viral possession he claims led to the accidental shooting of his wife, Joan, in 1951. In September of that year he had just returned from Mexico, overwhelmed with a 'feeling of doom and loss' when an attempt to shoot a glass balanced on Joan's head went tragically awry.[90] Burroughs later maintained that it was this event which initially propelled and later continued to shape his writing: 'the death of Joan brought me in contact with the invad-

89 McCarthy, 'Science & Fiction'.
90 William S. Burroughs, 'Introduction', in *Queer* (London: Picador, 1986), 17.

er, the Ugly Spirit, and maneuvered me into a lifelong struggle'.[91] He had encountered this Ugly Spirit previously, long before the shooting, when struck by the strange feeling of 'something in my being that was not me, and not under my control'.[92] Writing became a way to search for trajectories of escape, a war against controlling possession, a confrontation with the spirits that worked through him.

By 1959, the year in which he and Gysin discover the cut-up, Burroughs was preoccupied with 'incredible discoveries' involving a dark force that had taken up residence in his life. In correspondence from that year, he describes a particular vision: 'I looked in the mirror and saw my hands completely inhuman, thick, black-pink, fibrous, long white tendrils growing from the curiously abbreviated fingertips as if the finger had been cut off to make way for tendrils ... And Jerry, who was sitting across the room, said: "My God, Bill! What's wrong with your hands???"'[93] This vision of himself as a tendrillar plant-monster is supplemented on other occasions when, staring in mirrors, he turns into something else, something nonhuman. Others detect it, staring at him in restaurants.[94] But, at the same time, his friends comment on his 'growing invisibility'. In effect, Burroughs withdraws from communication at the same time as he communicates something from beyond. Arrested on drugs charges, police fail repeatedly to photograph him — when the pictures are developed, there's nothing there.[95] He is a vessel of both communication and excommunication. Burroughs describes the horror of something communicating, coming into visibility through him, while at the same time, as medium, he is self-negating, passing into imperceptibility. We are not just media, we are *weird media*; in Thacker's terms we see both more than we should and nothing at all. It is not positive knowledge of something coming through which we can reconcile with existing rational explanations, but rather the revelation of a gulf, an abyss between realities which is silent and opaque, which is not for

91 Ibid., 18.
92 Ibid., 16. Here he is referring to an incident that occurred when looking at Egyptian hieroglyphics.
93 William S. Burroughs, *Letters 1945–59* (London: Penguin Classics, 2009), 405.
94 Ibid., 418.
95 Ibid., 419.

us. It doesn't come across and speak — rather the ground drops away beneath us and we are at the limit of the human confronting a force which does not reciprocate, which is indifferent. This is the pure communication of a self-negating mediation in which senders and receivers dissolve and there is only the seething, horrifying middle.

Embedded in such horror, it is necessary to formulate a stratagematic mode of writing about media and photography that can be thought in terms of what McKenzie Wark calls 'low theory'. It is low because it is unhelpful, because it is 'negative', because it is used to reveal 'the void between what can be done and what is to be done.'[96] Thacker similarly argues that the dominant mode of philosophy, and by extension media and cultural theory more generally, serves three main functions: a therapeutic function, a descriptive function, and a hermeneutic function.[97] It helps us live better lives, it provides a truthful account of the world, it endows the world with meaning. However, for Thacker, like Wark, there is another kind of philosophical writing that does not simply aim to 'help a person understand something.' Indeed, he points to the importance of writing that, by any conventional academic assessment, is 'unhelpful', a low theory that 'works against the presuppositions of grand, systematic philosophy, composed as it is of fragments, aphorisms, stray thoughts.' Such writing has 'a subtractive rigour', what Nietzsche called the rigour of the 'unfinished thought'.

This book offers a low theory of photography in the form of multiple 'dispatches'. How might we define the dispatch? In journalism, a dispatch is a hastily composed report that responds directly to events of the present. Here, its urgency is dictated by its hopelessness. The dispatches that comprise this book are written without the triumphant advantage of historical reflection, without the opportunity for detailed analysis. Dispatches are fragmented, they refuse the logic demanded by synoptic perspective. There is, then, a sense of futility

---

96 McKenzie Wark, *The Beach Beneath the Street: The Everyday Life and Glorious Times of the Situationist International* (London: Verso, 2011), 156.

97 Eugene Thacker, 'The Sight of a Mangled Corpse: An Interview with Eugene Thacker', *Scapegoat: Architecture, Landscape, Political Economy* 5 (2013): 378–87. http://www.scapegoatjournal.org/docs/05/SG_Excess_378–387_F_Thacker. pdf. All citations of Thacker's work in this paragraph are from this source.

to the dispatch, it is written without the usual belief that communication will reveal some kind of order or meaning. Indeed, these dispatches do away with the pretence that the 'world' is 'real', just as they refuse the notion of an inaccessible reality, a presupposed world. Instead, they seek to communicate the world's unreality, even though they are communicated with the understanding that such efforts will always fail. Dispatches are operative constructs, tricks, stratagematic theory for producing intersections with an inhuman outside. In this, the dispatch is a bleak but necessary response to an indifferent world, to a middleness in which any-action-whatever has little determinable effect on the reality film.

Dispatch also suggests something functional and operational. To dispatch is to complete a task, to conduct something expeditiously and efficaciously without ceremony. It is suggestive of something procedural, technical, immanent to the vectors of mediation. Nietzsche's aphorisms, for example, can be described as dispatches. They are the result of experiments with early typewriter technology, experiments that led him to declare, 'Our writing tools are also working on our thoughts.'[98] Thirty or so years later, reflecting on his experience as a wireless correspondent, Marinetti wrote excitedly of new communications technologies that prompted a 'complete renewal of human sensibility', that prompted a wireless imagination.[99] It was the speed of such technologies, he insisted, that fully worked over the human. The wireless dispatch — a message sent in times of war, from the front line — expressed the newly 'rapid rhythm' of human life in which subjectivity was increasingly distributed and multiplied.[100] The dispatch is an exercise in decoding and scrambling subjectivity, forming relations with what Burroughs called 'external coordinates'.[101]

One of the most well known collections of dispatches was also written on the front line, even though they were reworked a decade

---

98 Nietzsche cited in Friedrich Kittler, *Gramophone, Film, Typewriter* (Stanford, California: Stanford University Press, 1999), 200.

99 Filippo Tommaso Marinetti, 'Destruction of Syntax — Wireless Imagination — Words-in-Freedom', in *Futurism: An Anthology*, ed. Lawrence Rainey et al. (New Haven and London: Yale University Press, 2009), 147.

100 Marinetti, 'Destruction of Syntax', 144.

101 Burroughs and Gysin, *The Third Mind*, 136.

later. Michael Herr's dispatches from the Vietnam War famously provided source material for *Apocalypse Now* and *Full Metal Jacket*. In
Herr's writing, where observation is never separate from participa-
tion, life on the front line is also never unmediated, never separate to
'movie-fed war fantasies' experienced by soldier and correspondent
alike.[102] The chaos and routine of war are both futile *and* seductive,
traumatic *and* glamorous:

> You don't know what a media freak is until you've seen the way a
> few of those grunts would run around during a fight when they
> knew that there was a television crew nearby; they were actu-
> ally making war movies in their heads... A lot of correspondents
> weren't much better. We'd all seen too many movies, stayed too
> long in Television City, years of media glut had made certain con-
> nections difficult.[103]

As he makes clear, the war correspondent is predisposed to ratio-
nalize these connections, to disentangle the visceral material reality
of war from its anesthetizing immaterial representations in various
media forms. It is the correspondent's job to understand the connections between image and event, between fiction and reality, and
having gained such an understanding to communicate the real experience of war to an audience back at home. But what Herr discovers
is that, as hard as a correspondent might try to pierce through processes of mediation and expose an apparently real war, there was only
ever a chaotic middle, a space and time that set 'your vision blurring,
images jumping and falling as though they were being received by a
dropped camera...'[104] In such a war, conventional journalism could
only take the world's unreality and 'turn it into a communication
pudding...'[105]

The dispatches gathered in the chapters that follow operate nega-
tively, they result from a dark intuition of something present but non-

---

102 Michael Herr, *Dispatches* (London: Picador, 2002), 198. Herr emphasizes the sig-
     nificance of the mythology of the Western (44).
103 Ibid., 212.
104 Ibid., 213.
105 Ibid., 220.

empirical. They are heretical in that the sanctity of the photographer is polluted, indeed the photographer exists only insofar as they are a mark of possession, rendered here in the form of what, after Deleuze and Guattari, might be called conceptual personae.[106] Collectively, they fabulate a different kind of photography, one in which the camera produces negative flashes that glitch the human and eventuate something other. This is photography's role in a War Universe.

---

106 Gilles Deleuze and Félix Guattari, *What is Philosophy?* (New York: Columbia University Press, 1994).

2 | Dispatches

2.1 | The Holiday Inn

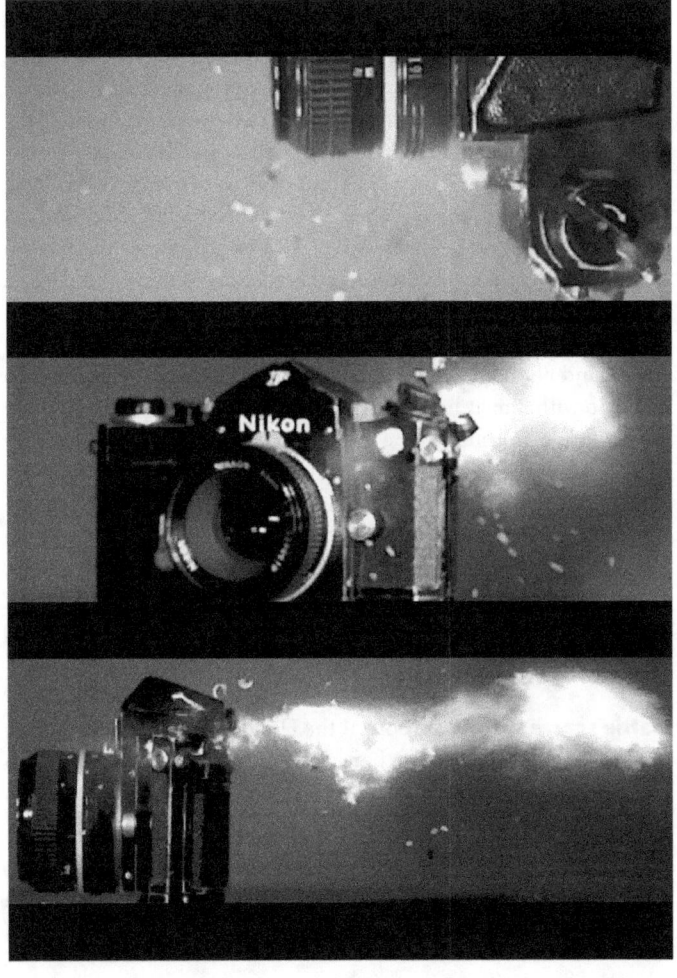

Goya at the Holiday Inn. Goya checks in and is irritated to see modern art and photography, doubles and parasites both, waiting at the desk. These hollow heads will conspire and ensure that, later on, it will be said with confidence that we know Goya, that he is common knowledge, just like we know and imagine war. We will empathize, fill his shoes, like Will Graham, profiler and hunter of psychopaths in NBC's *Hannibal*: 'This is my design'. Goya's *Disasters of War* (*Los Desastres de la Guerra*) will be contained, encrypted in the tradition and rhetoric we will, with hindsight, say he spawned. We will endlessly recycle these images. In them, we will see, as retrojected origin, the immediacy and directness of the war photographer, the clarity of the modern, critical eye undistracted by ornament. And we will see Jake and Dinos Goya repeat them in their noise and excess, as ambivalence and psychosis. Goya's restitution as demonic clown-king, furious forked entity, everywhere at once: I'm raping, I'm rending, castrating, crucifying. Meanwhile, Goya is bonkers in the bar, on a bender, entered and possessed by his legacy. These other Goyas, future Goyas, they've gagged him, blinded him and with so much work to do. Everything is the wrong way round! *I saw it*. Did I see it? Art and photography struggle into their flak jackets, and rush to catch up with him as he leaves the hotel in a flap. They already know that before his prints will be published, the camera will have been invented and will have premediated his foundational achievement, his decisive moment. Already, the unholy trinity hangs from the tree in Plate 39, assembled from mannequins, broken action men. Down shelled streets, Goya rushes or is pushed towards his inhuman end, Ligotti's puppet master defecting to the other side, to the '*secret too terrible to know*'. Goya, the first, the 'Black Source' — just a puppet, just a drone!¹

Battle scarred. The war room at the Holiday Inn. All the big name, big gun photojournalists are here. Their noses twitch, but there's no scent, no trail. For the moment, they can do nothing but wait. Wait,

---

1   Thomas Ligotti, *The Conspiracy Against the Human Race* (New York: Hippocampus Press, 2010), 18; Matthew Collings, *This is Modern Art* (London: Weidenfeld and Nicolson, 1999), 65.

drink hard liquor, smoke up a storm, practice their thousand-yard stare. Some of them — the freelancers, greenhorns without agency or newspaper sponsor — can't afford to stay here, but they stick to the sides, to the walls, hunting for lucky breaks. You need to start out naïve so that you can end up haunted. They know how it works. That's how you become damaged goods, that's how you get the look. The veterans in the room are self-consciously craggy, performatively pock marked like shrapnel damaged buildings, flamboyantly track marked like junkies living on the foil of war, mainlining the misery of human conflict. In the centre of the room's fug, Don McCullin and Robert King compare the talismanic cameras that hang from their necks. The best shot is the one that nearly kills you, but you need the right aura. In low tones, they each summon the apotropaic powers of their respective machine. Flak-magic. McCullin runs a gnarled finger across the dented pentaprism of his Nikon F, moving slowly down to the misshapen metal around the winder crank handle. This, an index of war, is 'the perfect imprint of an AK-47 round.' It embalms the instant, it is a matter of fact, contiguous with the truth. Undeterred, King conjures memorized trajectories through the air: a bullet lodged in the headrest of a car, a bullet that gives him a hot kiss on the ass, a bullet that lodges in his betacam. 'This bullet went through this camera', he murmurs. And, once again from the top, 'that's a Sony for you.' The wounded camera is reality correspondent — it corresponds, as Peirce put it, 'point by point to nature', to the syntax of the battle.[2]

Young man face scream. What can the war photographer do? What few affects define it in the vast forest of the warzone, pull all its organs and functions into being? Which prerecorded images does it use to synchronize itself with the world, singularize the rhythms of those invisible forces resonating in its body? Well, there is a stock photography of war, about war, enslaved to certain triggers. Start

2   Richard Parry, *Blood Trail: Shooting Robert King* (Revolver Entertainment, 2008); Don McCullin, *Unreasonable Behaviour: An Autobiography* (London: Vintage, 2002), 138; Charles Sanders Peirce, *Philosophical Writings of Peirce* (New York: Dover, 1955), 106.

somewhere stupid: 'Young man face scream — war conception'. This is the title of a stock photo accessible online at 123rf.com. A screaming man in a black t-shirt stands against a white background upon which crudely drawn fighter planes let loose their guns, bullets throwing up earth as they hit the ground behind him ('Similar' stock photos on offer on the same page include 'dangerous sniper with the rifle', 'young beautiful woman in t-shirt', 'close-up portrait of serious lady' and 'fashion young businessman black suit against dark background'). A simple scheme: War conception — spectacle of the horror, oh the inhumanity. Result — face scream. What are the options? To see and to document the horror that is seen. To compose, in an image, the effects produced by the forces of war. But — beyond the document, beyond effects — what of the forces themselves, invisible as they are; what of the violence that exceeds its spectacle? Deleuze lauded Francis Bacon for his response to this question. In a world conceived as unending war, unending suffering, insofar as it is conceived in terms of the bombardment of bodies by inhuman forces — and, as such, imperceptible, insensible and unliveable forces — the technical problem is to intimate the 'zone of indiscernibility' which the body becomes. Bacon immobilizes the body, the head, so that forces will not be registered only in the movements they effect. Bacon's heads are scrubbed, swept and smeared — convulsed and deformed in sensation but not transformed. Not transformed because they resolve into no specific form. To render sensation is to render the fury of force. These are heads thrust into the middle, between man and animal, human and inhuman. In them, faces are shrugged off and the meat swarms furiously. Such heads are way stations on the impossible path to the invisible. This is the art of the scream, in which the screamer 'cannot see … has nothing left to see'. Spectacle is to be 'scrambled', because in it forces must always remain invisible; in a combative 'act of vital faith', Bacon renounces spectacle for sensation. In this sense, to scream is to *believe*, not to see. Only then can a force be released which 'flushes out' and confronts the forces embattling the body on their own terms. So much for the man who painted those dreadful pictures. But what of photography? Must photography relinquish belief? Is photography always too late to the war?[3]

The frontest front line. The front line is the line of objective truth, the line at which history is encountered as it first unfolds. Real human experience, real people. In a short film produced for *The Times* promoting McCullin's return to war, the aged photographer is seen plodding through devastated Aleppo streets. Seventy-seven years old, he's had a bypass operation, a stroke, but he's back to where the bullets are flying, back to the zone demarcated from every other zone, back to the discrete world of war, separate to all other worlds. He wanted a mission, and for his sins they gave him one. At first, he's like a kid at Christmas — gleefully crossing over the border, eager to lend words of advice to young freelancers. This is the real thing, with none of the cozy but blinkered restrictions of embedment: no 'strategic communications' directed by Central Command, no indemnification releases, no escort. Almost immediately, though, McCullin's project stalls, his camera falters. It happens late in the afternoon when returning to the abandoned government building that rebels have made their base of operations. As his car travels through what remains of an avenue of trees, McCullin leans his head against the window, closing his eyes against the sun. Without warning, he is overcome by an intense surge of kaleidoscopic colours and complex patterns that burst behind his eyelids. A frenetic slide projector pulses out abstract images, flickering in polychromatic HP5, vibrantly colourized Tri-X. As the car makes it way out of the avenue, the power of this vision ends as abruptly as it had begun. In the days that follow this penetrating but unexplained occurrence, the front line seems somehow to lose its specificity, its power to communicate. For McCullin, the world of documentary realism is revealed as a dreamscape, a world of real fictions — real, just not yet actualized, virtual forces that condition and aestheticize all forms of communication. It is, he says, 'very, very bizarre, very strange…like being in a Fellini film.' Stricken with photographer's block, McCullin's images now seem nothing more

---

3   Gilles Deleuze, *Francis Bacon: The Logic of Sensation* (London and New York: Continuum, 2004), 59–62.

than shadows of other images, not quite visible, flickering moments of enlightenment generated by inverse processes of endarkenment. He feels weightlessly tethered to a world he cannot capture in its totality, always already embedded. Pierced and punctured by unseen vectors, he is a photographic Wound Man scrabbling to document other front lines that remain ungraspable, that remain impossible to confront.[4]

Venus or something. *D'you know what the man's saying? Do you? This is dialectics. It's very simple dialectics — one through nine, no maybes no supposes no fractions. You can't travel in space, you can't go out into space y'know without like y'know... er, with fractions. What are you gonna land on, one quarter? Three eighths? What are you gonna do when you go from here to Venus or something? That's dialectic physics, okay? Dialectic logic is, there's only love and hate. You either love someone, or you hate 'em.* So says Dennis Hopper's far out photographer, festooned with cameras, too long in the jungle. William Burroughs, less festooned but further out, identifies Venus as home to the power he named Control. In 1968 he made contact with this entity, through the rather unsatisfactory offices of Willy Deiches and Brenda Dunks, two ex-IBM employees become Nova agents, residents of Fulham Road, London. For a fee of 12 shillings per question, Deiches and Dunks submitted Burroughs's questions to Control via computer-assisted link involving newspaper cuttings and various mysterious procedures. Interpreting the responses, Burroughs became sceptical — why would Control answer? Well, perhaps Control plays ball to discover what you know, what you give away in your questioning. In any case, whatever the value this polite Q&A, this genteel messaging to and fro, might have had in 1968, it must certainly be a redundant form of communication

---

4   Hattie Garlick and Johnny Howorth, *Don's Last War* (*The Times*, 2012) https://vimeo.com/56683563; Anthony Loyd, 'McCullin's Last War', *The Times Magazine*, 29 December (2012), 8–19; US Department of Defense, 'Embedment Manual', in *Embedded: The Media at War in Iraq*, ed. Bill Katovsky and Timothy Carlson (Guildford, CT: The Lyons Press, 2004), 401–17; John Geiger, *Chapel of Extreme Experience: A Short History of Stroboscopic Light and the Dream Machine* (Brooklyn: Soft Skull Press, 2003), 11; John Geiger, *Nothing Is True Everything Is Permitted: The Life of Brion Gysin* (New York: The Disinformation Company, 2005), 160.

today, when Control has passed fully into the vector, into the middle, preempting the temporality of the message. The power of Control, it seems, is not dialectical but ecological, processual. It is, then, necessary to find weapons appropriate to the war, to confront Control on its own terms. Old dualisms won't help us here.[5] Communication must instead take the form of experiments with non-dialectical difference, a difference that is not separate to an other, but flickering parts of a single substance, a single unstable Real.

Secreted like beetles. 1993, Sarajevo. Robert King, fool in fatigues, is hovering again like an embarrassing fart in the foyer of the Holiday Inn. He catches a glimpse of Sontag — fed up of just *witnessing,* for Christ's sake — discussing her plans for staging a production of *Waiting for Godot* in the city ('something that would exist only in Sarajevo... No longer can a writer consider that the imperative task is to bring the news to the outside world. The news is out'). King doesn't feel Lucky at the moment, even though he's the star of his own film. He wants to be on the *inside* of this scene, goddamn, but he can't get a room. What a romantic. What an insect. 'Why', asked Robert Fisk, same time, same place, 'have so many of us written so many words about these often grubby hotels when epic tragedies outside their doors should have made such reports both tasteless and inappropriate?' Answering himself, he moralizes 'by doing so, we help to romanticise ourselves'. The real world lies beyond the foyer while the press stay inside, 'secreted like beetles'. But, really, today, the world has dismantled the walls and *vectoralized* the hotel, like the torrent of blood bursting through elevator doors in Kubrick's *The Shining*. It's the same 'space', no difference. Here is the front line, blood trailed deep inside the complex, and here is the secret meaning of what will come to be called 'embedment'. In embedment, the world explodes the logic of the 'assignment'. Roger Caillois' remarkable thesis on animal mimicry and crypsis is that it is no strategic camouflage oriented towards a dog-eat-dog reality but rather that the organism is fascinated, seduced and *trapped* by its environment, victim to the

---

5   Brion Gysin and William S Burroughs, 'Control...Control?' in Gysin, *Here to Go,* 215–29; Deleuze and Guattari, *A Thousand Plateaus,* 23.

'veritable lure' of 'dark space'. The background — penetrative and engulfing — assimilates the animal and not vice versa: 'Space', says Caillois, 'seems to constitute a will to devour. Space chases, entraps, and digests [organisms] in a huge process of phagocytosis. Then, it ultimately takes their place'. In sinking into the epic tragedy of media matter, the cryptic is drained of independent life: 'I am referring, so to speak, to the *inertia of the elan vital*'. Embedment is essentially a counterinsurgent practice through which the third estate's 'insurgency' is weaponized against itself. All populating this environment are reassigned as puppets because their affective capacities get immediately conscripted into the drama and battlefield of a sublime, oceanic force of mediation: 'So', as J.G. Ballard comments, 'you got this kind of drowned world where we all suddenly become rather silent aquatic creatures floating in this space, unaware of the direction of the current that was carrying us along'. King's failure to drown, to float convincingly, is in fact his principle virtue. Blast *McCullin*. Bless *Shooting Robert King*.[6]

The Hunger. In contemporary media ecologies, we succumb and volunteer ourselves to a theatre of operations in which our role is input and output. In this Cailloisian space, there is a terrifying proximity and indistinction of everything, precipitated by the fractalization and informationalization of the self in 'immanent promiscuity'. The romanticized reality film of the war photographer seeds the everyday banality of the social media user: 'Each new user', William Merrin comments, 'confident in their control as they construct and daily manipulate their promotional self, is, like Caillois's insects, caught by its own spell, trapped by their own incantation'. From 1935–36 (coinciding with Caillois' mimicry essay), Max Ernst produced several

---

6 Susan Sontag, 'Godot Comes to Sarajevo', *New York Review of Books*, 21 October 1993; Robert Fisk, 'Please, Sam, we'll pay you not to play it again', *The Independent*, 2 June 1993; Roger Caillois, *The Edge of Surrealism* (Durham and London: Duke University Press, 2003), 100; J.G. Ballard, "Not entirely a journey without maps': J.G. Ballard on The Atrocity Exhibition', in *Extreme Metaphors: Interviews with J.G. Ballard 1967–2008,* ed. Simon Sellars and Dan O'Hara (London: Fourth Estate, 2012), 455; Jacqui Morris, *McCullin* (British Film Company, 2012); Parry, *Blood Trail.*

paintings entitled 'Garden Aeroplane Trap' (*Jardin gobe-avions*). In-spired by C.J. Kresz's 1820 treatise on bird-trapping techniques, Ernst speculated on the strange fate of transcendent aerial power, death from above neutralized by odd artificial landscapes, garden-like an-gular wooden boxes or stone terraces. Aeroplanes — more like woe-fully twisted planes folded in paper by children than sophisticated killing machines — appear to have been subject to the encroachment of a peculiar natural menace, a nature which itself is transformed by the contact. Sprouting from them, or engulfing them, are colourful plant-like excrescences, sinister bouquets, occasionally resembling fly-traps, crustaceans or insectile forms. Here is a mutual engulfment or interpenetration in process, a collision of natures. As Ernst himself comments, here are 'voracious gardens in turn devoured by a vegeta-tion that springs from the debris of trapped airplanes'. Or, in Jeanette Baxter's words, 'the organic devours the inorganic which devours the organic'. Here is an inhuman, chaotic, hungry space, a mediatic space of possibility for weird, irruptive events awaiting their pre-photographic stabilization (these are gardens, if weird gardens). It is though in the after-image of such an event — in which a multiplicity of connectings and transformative devourings are briefly subject to a strange kind of illumination — that we might catch a glimpse of its vectoral contours.[7]

Ugly pictures. Robert King's room at the Holiday Inn. McCul-lin and Goya have just left, the three of them having spent the day ritualistically drinking Martell Cordon Bleu, smashing mirrors, and — stripped down to their underwear — weeping, with extreme prejudice. The room is now littered with empty bottles, makeshift ashtrays overflow, a burnt odour drifts from the en suite. Ensconced in this grime, King is hunched over a small portable television on which, amidst considerable static, Michael Parkinson (doyen of British talkshow hosts) interviews the war photographer William

7   William Merrin, 'Myspace and Legendary Psychasthenia', *Media Studies 2.0*, 14 September 2007, http://mediastudies2pointo.blogspot.co.uk/2007/09/myspace-and-legendary-psychasthenia.html; Jeannette Baxter, *J.G. Ballard's Sur-realist Imagination: Spectacular Authorship* (Surrey: Ashgate, 2009), 83; Wark, *Tel-esthesia*, 68, 33, 35.

S Burroughs. The television signal is intermittent and occasionally drops out entirely, so King is forced to continually adjust the coat hanger that stands in for an aerial. In tight close up, made closer still by King's proximity to the bulbous screen, Burroughs ignores Parky's sycophantic line of questioning and addresses the camera directly: *You think you know what death is, Robert Oppenheimer... you think you are death, but you don't know death, you Ugly American shit. Not until you've seen the pictures. It's complicated is what it is. Death is your crash landing.* WHEEEEEEE... BLINDING FLASH. *That's when your death shows itself... look around. It's gray, like newsprint. That flash, that crash, that was the Old Photographer right there, working for the control machine. Here it is, I wrote it: 'He knows that* DEATH *is the picture of Death. Of your death. This is proved by the fact that there is somebody there to take the picture. Show someone the picture of his death and you kill him. Fear is the pictures of your fear'. In a newspaper, it'll kill you, kill hundreds — terrible accidents, crashes, a fire here and there, a school shooting. It's an old, old trick — seen it a hundred times. Done it a few times myself, actually. Here are the editors: 'Go out and get the pictures. The ugly pictures. If you can't find them make them'. I know newspapers... I know editors, Ugly Americans, old photographers, they're all instruments of Control. All pictures are war pictures. See, me, I don't work for Control. Not from around here. An* intrusion *is what I am. Got a different kind of* focus. *Gather round, see this scrapbook... Like to see where this goes? Intersect with these coordinates? Now, listen for the click...* King's tense grip on the aerial momentarily tremors and Burroughs is immediately replaced with noise.[8]

Embedded. Later, King assembles documents that he believes might constitute a photographic weapon. Kneeling on the floor in the centre of the room, he arranges images torn from old magazines, advertisements and brochures: (1) photograph of Hitler's bathtub; (2) poster of James Woods as Richard Boyle in El Salvador; (3) nomenclature of Canon F-1; (4) photograph of a blast furnace in Mag-

---

8   Morris, *McCullin*. See William S. Burroughs and Malcolm McNeill, 'The Unspeakable Mr Hart', *Cyclops* 1–4 (July–October 1970); William Burroughs, *Ah Pook Is Here and Other Texts* (London: John Calder, 1979), 33, 34.

nitogorsk; (5) photograph of glamorous women in black fire masks at the entrance to an air raid shelter; (6) reproduction of an image from Max Ernst's 'Garden Aeroplane Trap' series; (7) photograph of a car accident, New York, 1965; (8) poster of Nick Nolte as Russell Price in Nicaragua; (9) nomenclature of Nikon F2 and MD-2 motor drive; (10) panorama of Yosemite Valley. King has no interest in how these image documents might be interpreted. He has come to realize that they do not add up to anything fixed or comprehensive but act instead as a collision of interrelated processes and patterns, throwing open a series of potentials, the vectoral energies of which might be exploited according to different, wholly oppositional, trajectories.

More elegance. After the correspondents had prepared the city for its liberation, Miller had received a telegram from Vogue with a new assignment. She was to document the reemergence of haute couture, cover the signs of a new season as it springs forth. Glamour from the ruins, that kind of thing. Her initial efforts had been met with a less than enthusiastic response. MORE ELEGANCE, instructed a second telegram from the magazine's editor. The world is waiting to see what the city will produce post-oppression. Photograph the new collections, the openings that open onto a post-war world. Irritated at these instructions from London, Miller had concluded that her editor had little idea what was happening at the front line — the London office didn't seem to understand that the war is far from over. Miller had, though, picked up on rumours of a show embedded within the war itself, a show of real elegance. Though she hadn't heard from him in weeks, she had become convinced that her lover, the British surrealist and *camoufleur,* Roland Penrose, was behind this new collection. Following the collapse of the Industrial Camouflage Research Unit, the company he had established with a group of fellow artists at the outbreak of war, Penrose had taken on a lecturing role for the War Office, teaching the theory and practice of camouflage to the Home Guard. To demonstrate camouflage in action, the slides for his lectures would often include an image of Miller lying naked on the lawn, covered in green paint and netting. Training in the strategic use of colour and texture, obliterative shading, disruptive patterns, and the elimination of cast shadows can 'teach a man how to control his tone', he often said. Penrose's lectures did not simply address concealment though, they also dealt with deception, misdirection and bluff. In this, he turned to 'nature as a guide', to the natural strategies of deceptive markings, deceptive behaviour. As a committed painter, he had in the past shown little interest in photography, but in his recent letters Penrose had increasingly fixated on Caillois's assertion that morphological mimicry is 'genuine photography... photography of shape and relief, on the order of objects and not of images'. The show was not difficult for Miller to track down. Following a few enquiries with her contacts at various fashion houses, she was escorted to the show's front line in the hills surrounding the Holiday Inn. It seemed the collection was designed to be viewed from a distance: high off the ground, and through a telephoto lens or telescopic sight. Miller climbed into the imitation tree provided as observation post and shinnied her way to the top where the extended focal length of her lens picked out the catwalk — a rough clearing in the distance. For a while she could see only the obvious decoys: the dummy photographers crouched in the scrub wearing dummy flak jackets holding dummy cameras lodged with dummy bullets. Aside from these static forms, the show's models appeared to be embedded to the point of disappearance. The catwalk was empty. And then, gradually, as the hours passed, Miller began to perceive the vague outline of familiar forms and faces shuttling along its length: McCullin, King, Goya, three-dimensional reproductions, sculpture photographs.[9]

Crossroads. Beneath tattered clouds, beneath the moon, Don strode into the clearing and stood at the crossroads. How legends are born, how they live — an offering is made. You're supposed to bury something. If you bury a suicide or a criminal at such a place, you can make a zombie. For instance. Don thinks, paces a while. Empties his pockets. In the end, Don buries himself, sort of. He buries his past. To be reborn to a new kind of assignment. Reborn to the war.

---

9   Burke, *Lee Miller*, 235; Ronald Penrose, *Home Guard Manual of Camouflage* (London: George Routledge and Sons, 1941); Peter Forbes, *Dazzled and Deceived: Mimicry and Camouflage* (New Haven and London: Yale University Press, 2009), 135.

Reborn to the middle of everything. And he will stand there, he will look around. He will see, he will not look away and he will believe. How a legend is born. Strike a deal. Go back into the forest and take the shots. Legendary, ugly shots. Double-page spreads. Covers.

Be the war. 'Be the change you want to see in the world', Gandhi said. But Don wanted to *be the war*. Exercising his magic powers: 'This may sound ridiculous', Don says, 'but I know that I have a perception of coincidences which has allowed me to get close to certain situations and come away alive'. And how exactly did you come by these skills, Mr. McCullin?[10]

A split second. First of all, he would dip in, get his shots and then, he would run! Run like the wind, thinking 'Got it! Got it!' But it wasn't enough — he began to need to stay. You couldn't really take anything away. The point was *being* there. You cannot disrupt an act of true worship. Longer and longer. Weeks, even. Till even the warriors started thinking, 'What the fuck?' It was out of time, whether the Congo, 'Nam, Cambodia, El Salvador, the Lebanon, just out of history. All one war, one universe. One landscape. And, then later, everything remains so clear, every detail, like the individual leaves of a tree or droplets of a river. Don remembers every little fragment, crystalline, every shutter speed and aperture.[11]

Free-shooter. In 1990, Burroughs collaborated with Robert Wilson and Tom Waits in the production of *The Black Rider,* a stage musical based on a German folktale of the supernatural, *Der Freischütz.* Burroughs wrote the libretto and, talking guns with pals at his home in Kansas in the year of its premiere, he explicitly connects the project to his conception of the 'war universe'. What is the war universe? It's the only game in town — ceaseless hostilities between an unseen ad-

---

10 Morris, *McCullin.*

11 'I took a picture of a grenade thrower. It was 250 f.8, because he was throwing a grenade, and I still managed to stop the hand grenade in the air. Except in the split second after I took the picture, a bullet completely destroyed his hand. He had a hand like a cauliflower, and he was weeping, and I photographed him crying.' Don McCullin, in Morris, *McCullin.*

versary — an invasive force, an Ugly Spirit — and all the forces you can muster. Everything hinges on drawing out the Ugly Spirit, rendering him visible, because his powers hinge on obscurity. He thrives in fog. And where do you find him? Always between worlds, at the crossroads, at the intersection. He'll show himself for sure because he's always more than ready to make a deal. How does Burroughs's libretto relate to this? A file clerk, looking to step up to the mark and win his lady love, is compelled to prove himself as a hunter but can't shoot for shit. The only way to do it? He has to go down to the forest, find some lonely crossroads and enter a pact with something real ugly. Once in the forest, the magic bullets he's granted seem to fulfil his wishes — can't miss — but you know only the first few shots are free. It's him being triggered, and, when it counts, he can't pull away. Addiction, that's the real deal. Take the shot, destroy the reason you did it all for in the first place, and you're delivered right back to the Ugly Spirit. Any deal you make at the crossroads — you pay it all back, none of it was ever really yours. Hit the mark, hit the dark. That's the thing about skills of the middle — no such thing as free-shooting. The trick, Burroughs tells his pals, is to know your fate. Name your horror. It's all there, at the intersection. It's where everything is written, edited, spliced. Pay attention, watch it happen. You may make a difference, you may force a change, but you've got to know how things happen. Ports of entry accessed only by getting out of the way of yourself.[12]

'Endarkenment'. This is the story a Legend tells itself in the small hours: It was a gay old time, but it had to end. Don, febrile, turned his back on the luminous darkness of the Holiday Inn, the amphitheatre of war. Somerset beckoned, with all its trees and its flowers, its springs and its summers — healing had to happen. But England called him back for judgement, for the trial and the sentence awaiting him. In his body's cloaca, the darkness and the fever hitched a ride. Noisy ghosts installed in the filing cabinet. 'Sometimes it felt like I was carrying pieces of human flesh back home with me, not nega-

---

12   'The War Universe', in *Burroughs Live: The Collected Interviews of William S. Burroughs 1960–1997*, ed. Sylvère Lotringer (New York: Semiotext(e), 2001), 735–46.

tives. It's as if you are carrying the suffering of the people you have photographed'. One in the morning, always that time, waking in a cold sweat from nightmares of imprisonment, beatings, old wounds itching. Where once his mission was to be unflinching, absolutely non-moral — straddle the forcefield and make with the vectoral magic, take the pictures-from-which-one-must-not-look-away — now *all he seems to do is flinch,* dwell on the moral, dwell on the guilt. A gunshot rings out like a bell — who hunts in the middle of the night? Photography isn't anything to do with looking or seeing. It's a feeling, the kind of feeling you can never shake. If your business is this kind of photography it's a stew in which you're always going to cook. The feeling that endures is the tearing of the bullet, the bullet with your name on it, that one your camera took instead of your face. The bullet that was your final press pass — to the battlefield of your soul. Final cover story — the Legend is driven mad. The fly twitches in the web. Operation Wandering Soul lifted out of 'Nam and brought home to Avalon. Portable darkness. Don came back to heal, but has found only winter, only chill, only the ghost of coincidence past. 'This may sound ridiculous …' Only Goya corralling the other larvae in the furthest rooms of his home, rattling through the negatives, scattering the butchered flesh, the instruments of a surgery of coincidence. At home, he was always the evacuee. A peace sentence. Photography always leaves you in the dark.[13]

Ceasefire. The bar in the Holiday Inn. Goya sits with the television crew that has been listlessly following him around these past weeks. They continue to await his miserable war stories. Tales of Saragossa. Memories of Napoleon. Summary executions. Assaults on the body. Something. Anything. Yet Goya remains silent. Miller, the director of the crew, tries to suppress her growing frustration. After days of nothing but desultory wandering, the subject of her programme has still yet to come up with the goods. And now that fighting has moved to within one block of the hotel, she knows that the city's ever more abstract geography of bombed out department stores and apartments, its shattered offices and banks, will provide an ideal

---

13 Morris, *McCullin.*

backdrop to Goya's delirious inventory of atrocities. If only her star would communicate.

Misfire. Darkness. A black tomb, a black box. Hidden down here, a decomposing corpse lies on its side. Rather than acting simply as a symbol of man's inhumanity to man, this corpse is raising itself up in a final act of speechless communication. In its hand the corpse clutches a sign on which is written 'Nada'. Threatening faces leer in the shadows. *Nada,* or *Nothing,* was the original caption Goya gave to this image, Plate 69 of his *Disasters of War.* The words 'Ello dirá' (which can be translated as 'Time will tell', or 'We shall see') were posthumously added to the caption at the time of its publication. As Juliet Wilson-Bareau describes it, the original title was simply too ni-hilistic, too pessimistic, for the Academy which first published the work, and the institution felt obliged to give the image a marginal sense of hope, an affirmative spin. Nada is something negative, an absence, and last words should point to form not void. In Conrad's *Heart of Darkness,* Marlow saves Kurtz's wife the trauma of recount-ing the words that so haunt him — 'The horror! The horror!' — by saying that it was her name choked in her husband's last breath. Life can't end on a downer, a sigh, with the 'lethargy of discontent'. The void, the inaccessible, must remain just that. Even Rustin Cohle, one time cosmic pessimist of HBO's *True Detective,* ends up Enlightened by comparison: 'once there was only dark. You ask me, the light's winning.' The void is reduced to familiar form, communication tri-umphs. It's not the lack of form, of order, it's just that we haven't recognized it yet. Too complex, y'see. But what if the philosophi-cal negativeness of Nada, the failure or refusal to take on any *form* at all, was generative in itself? What if there was a mode of media-tion through which it became possible to communicate with 'that which is, by definition, inaccessible'. Not to represent, not to reduce to something familiar, but, as Eugene Thacker has it, to communicate 'inaccessibility in and of itself'. What if there was something other than communication as we know it, something other to the repres-sive control of communication's circuit, to its cycle of production? What if, to quote Deleuze, there were 'circuit breakers, so that we can elude control'? Photography, a matter of endarkenment rather than

Enlightenment, possesses a weird intimacy with forces that remain voided. Nada is the pessimistic function of photography, a sorrow at the form of communication itself. Nada: 'the right to say nothing'.[14]

Arcanum of the Exploded Camera. Nada is also the nomadic hero of John Carpenter's *They Live,* the nothing who stumbles, through a lens darkly, over the alien conspiracy which controls the population of Los Angeles, perhaps the world, by means of subliminal media messages: 'They are safe as long as they are not discovered. That is their primary method of survival. Keep us asleep, keep us selfish, keep us sedated.' Only ye who are lost, ye of little consequence, nothing to say, nowhere to go, ye who intrude and who irritate, may don the dark glass and see, see to dismantle the faces and pry out the teeming alien rhizome. This, our Tarot of the Dark Glass, Arcanum of the Exploded Camera: Muybridge the Magician, Goya the Hanged Man, McCullin the Devil, King the Fool, Miller the Empress, Burroughs without Name.

Nature trail. For the forester, von Uexküll says, the oak tree is a 'few cords of wood'. For the little girl, the tree has a 'danger tone', thronging as it is with vile gnomes. For the fox, owl or squirrel harboured in its bole and branches, the tree sounds a 'protection' or 'supporting' tone. The ant perceives only the bark which is its hunting ground. What does the legendary devil, McCullin, perceive of the tree and the forest? Of what miracles of affect do his sensory instruments consist? Or maybe it's simple, perhaps only a few affects, like the tick or the fly? 'Nothing but a few signs like stars in an immense black night'. A light sleeper, he waits in his room in the Holiday Inn like

---

14 See Philip Hofer's introduction to the 1967 Dover edition of Francisco Goya's *The Disasters of War,* and Juliet Wilson-Bareau's essay included in the catalogue for the 1998 exhibition of the work at London's Hayward Gallery (*Disasters of War: Callot Goya Dix,* London: Cornerhouse Publications, 29–40); Eugene Thacker, *Cosmic Pessimism* (Minneapolis: Univocal, 2015), 5; Eugene Thacker, 'Dark Media', in *Excommunication: Three Inquiries in Media and Mediation,* ed. Alexander Galloway, Eugene Thacker and McKenzie Wark (Chicago and London: University of Chicago Press, 2014), 81, 96; Gilles Deleuze, *Negotiations 1972–1990* (New York: Columbia University Press, 1995), 175, 129.

the tick waiting on the end of its high twig for the sweet scent of a passing mammal's sweat, the warmth of blood. The tick lives to drop and burrow, for the sweat, flesh and blood of it all. The snout of the photographer-tick, for its part, is twitching with the sweat of fear... anticipative, sensing a decisive moment in the offing, imagining — *feeling* — the intersections of a magical web of coincidence. The tick can wait on its twig for decades — shuts down, nothing doing — but McCullin is a faster animal, feeding twice a year. Two wars a year. McCullin, tugging on his flak jacket, is really 'McCullin', the signature, sprayed around the perimeters of a warzone. The McCullin sensorium is co-constituted with the warzone, embedded, burrowing. McCullin and his war become together, each harbours the other's otherness, the likeness of the other. McCullin has the tone, the image of the zone, painted inside his nervous system. McCullin is a tone, a singularization of tone, a biologic film which expresses a tribe, a photoist operation which is a kind of surgery, a kind of cutting — coincidence butchery, intersection art, crossroads voodoo. Photography will not renounce its share of the violence. A thread of blood, circling, patrolling these pre-haunted and pre-damned images, all down the long, long years from Goya. A Collection of Dead Men. This is Bad. This is the Truth. Nada. Nada Truth. The hazard of war photoism is the bullet lodged in the camera, the exploded camera, the camera which breaks with the blood trail, like third nature breaks with second, to experiment with affects, composing a new kind of music. Music of the vector. The camera which sees nothing and believes it. Music of sighs and screams. Opening line of *Waiting for Godot*: 'Nothing to be done'. The sun is high, blazing through clouds of dust which stir in the breeze, the warrior's hand releases the grenade, the bullet is on its way, Don clicks, stops time, time starts, grenade, bullet and flesh crash together, nature is screaming, crying, suffering, Don stalks it, takes it, takes it. Style, singularization, haecceity, the crystal of the Holiday Inn. The tick's trick.[15]

---

15   Jakob von Uexküll, *A Foray into the Words of Animals and Humans: With a Theory of Meaning* (Minneapolis: University of Minnesota Press, 2010), 128–29; Gilles Deleuze and Claire Parnet, *Dialogues II* (London: Continuum, 2006), 61.

A typical world city. In Ballard's short story, 'War Fever', Beirut is a designed experience, engineered and modulated: 'Everything, even the McDonald's. The UN architects designed it as a typical world city — a Hilton, a Holiday Inn, a sports stadium, shopping malls. They brought in orphaned teenagers from all over the world, from every race and nationality. To begin with we had to prime the pump — the NCOs and officers were all UN observers fighting in disguise. But once the engine began to turn, it ran with very little help'. This is the city as alchemy of aggression, as 'war laboratory', in which war is instigated and contained as an affective virus, a phenomenon of belief, constantly mutating. The city at war, so you don't have to be. Containment affords the luxury of scrutiny and manipulation, perfecting the art of pre-photography, of affective tone and resonance, of flows of weapons and media ('Just a few atrocity photographs...'). Plenty of work for a legion of picture makers and poster boys and girls. Ballard's protagonist, Ryan, dreams of a cease-fire, and, when this is scuppered by the 'peace-keepers', and he discovers the world outside the city has been at peace for decades, his dream turns to unleashing the virus upon the outside world. But Ballard's fiction is, of course, already outpaced by reality itself. The walls came down and the virus of war was loosed some time ago. Post-ideological power — the disjunctive synthesis of Security and Terror that characterizes life today — already opened the bloodgates and transformed the world into experiment, the cosmos into laboratory of contagions. The forest. War ecology. Welcome to the Holiday Inn. Stay smart.[16]

Fly on the wall. Robert King is a fly on the walls of the Holiday Inn, a fly with a feeling eye. The Inn is an intersection of strands of a spider-city building webs. The operationalization of the city as designed experience commandeers powers of mediation to direct perception and capture attention. The spider creeps up on you *because* it left you the room to wriggle. Magic techniques of camouflage, dazzle and adjacency. This seductive web, this weird garden, is voracious but recessive, inconspicuous. The spider-city is evil media, grey, in shadow. Its power is anticipatory; in its body it already carries King's code as its

---

16   J.G. Ballard, *War Fever* (London: HarperCollins, 1990).

very own potential, a likeness of his body, eye and camera. The city is inhuman. The city is a photography-trap. It makes the pictures you want to take, it lays the blood trail, and then sits and waits. It makes the world for capture. The warzone captures and devours the unwary photographer. If King's cicerone is the devil McCullin, King is the fool who steps afterwards, carefree, into an abyss already strung with nets. You can only fall so far before you suffer forces of adhesion, before you are *connected*. The spider builds its web as it does for invisibility; having stolen the likeness of the photographer's sensorium, it knows in its very body how to elude detection, how to pass itself off as Truth, as abyss, as mere *spectacle* of horror. And what of King? What are his chances? This is the crux — can the fool, falling, strip the city back to its larvae, the weird garden back to its roots, and map its forces in order to make his whatever weapon? Fictions of every kind. Photography at its fabulatory middle. Refrains and the noise that dissolves them. The magic formula, *solve et coagula*. The secret, larval compost-space of photography as oceanic, network horror of life. These are his chances. They are ours, too.[17]

---

17   Fuller and Goffey, *Evil Media*.

2.2 | CSI **Düsseldorf**

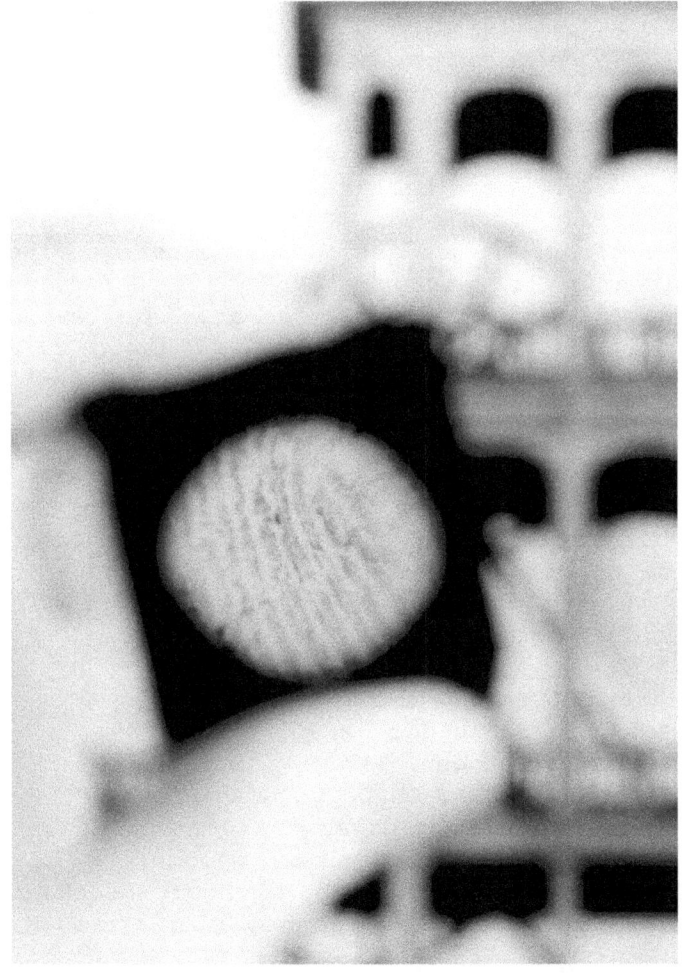

The following fragments originate in leaked classified files. Little has ever emerged about the broader motivations and machinations of the enigmatic police cabal known, where it has even been acknowledged, as Sektion Null, but what is clear is that the files in question all relate to an operation with the code name Documenta, relating to surveillance of photographers Bernd and Hilla Becher. The Bechers adopted an influential methodology for the photographing of industrial structures (viz. the Düsseldorf School), structuring their exhibited work according to a number of ideas about typological organization. Operation Documenta appears to have been conducted over a five year period, roughly 1967 to 1972 (dates have largely been expunged from the leaked files as made available to us, but they seem to concentrate on the period '68-'69), and involved interviews, wire taps, letter intercepts, covert recordings, house searches, general surveillance and more specialized infiltration and dreamwork. As far as possible, we have arranged the fragments chronologically, with the exception of the most recent document, a Sektion Null memo, which we present first.

NONDISCLOSABLE MEMO
To: Cptn Schneider
Date: 13 October, 1972
Subject: OPERATION DOCUMENTA
This office is pleased to report that Operation Documenta has been a complete success. We recommend Special Agent Szeemann be awarded the high commendation (though,

of course, he will remain unaware of his work for this office). As you know, the aim of the operation was to instigate a general perceptual shift whereby the investigation led by Hilla and Bernd Becher would be safely recuperated as art. We are now able to report that this endeavour has been entirely successful. The exhibition, entitled 'Interrogation of Reality -- Picture Worlds Today' and held in Kassel earlier this year, exceeded our expectations. Indeed, it is no exaggeration to describe it as a blockbuster of sublime spectacle. Accordingly, although photographic excerpts from the Bechers' enquiries had already been released publically, in New York and elsewhere, the scale and international ambition of this show (200+ artists, 1000+ exhibits), and its success at bringing together values previously deemed experimental, radical or counter-cultural (utopia, play, science-fiction), marks a decisive shift in power relations. While the end of the exhibition marks the formal conclusion of this operation, it is the belief of this office that events now set in motion will securitize the ecological circumstances in which the Bechers' investigation takes place. We might imagine an industry of large scale international biennials, managed by artist-curators, which remains safely regulated by a strong art market. However, beyond such speculation, it is clear that the current trajectory of the Bechers' investigation is now firmly associated with minimal and concept art, and that public perception of its future development will be aligned to these aesthetics. You are advised to refer to the Assets Inventory for further background.

Shift report, undercover agent *(Unsigned, but we have reason to believe the agent's name to be Voss and his report to have been made in late '67/early '68)*
After lunch, and a discussion with Hilla about the Bechers' investigations, I helped set up the ladders and then I watched out for them both while they poked around in some dangerously toxic nooks and crannies around the plant. She told me that their work meant being surrounded by dead or dying beasts, primeval arrangements. This tangle of technological corpses feels ancient even as it remains unbelievably precise, so it seems appropriate to take a cue from the ordering systems of natural sciences. When you arrive at the scene (like a crime scene, Hilla said) you're aware that nature is slowly encroaching, you can feel the hard forms...becoming soft.[1] Industrial nature, for the Bechers, is neither good nor bad. They have assumed a forensic attitude which resists, or at least attempts to re-

---

1   Bernd Becher: 'even though it looks so primeval and jungle-like, there is an unbelievable precision to an industrial plant that cannot be represented by painting.' Cited in Susanne Lange, *Bernd and Hilla Becher: Life and Work,* trans. Jeremy Gaines (Cambridge, MA: MIT Press, 2007), 204. Hilla Becher refers to the industrial plants as 'the scene of the crime' (cited in ibid., 213), and contends that 'a blast furnace is like a living creature. Barely has it ceased to function than it dies. It is dead and decays and seldom mummifies' (cited in ibid., 209). Writing in her diary about a visit, in 1983, to a plant in Alabama, Hilla Becher notes: 'The plant is completely dead and looks like a thousand-year-old temple in the jungle, but everything is still there in original condition, it is only that nature is encroaching slowly and the hard forms are slowly becoming soft' (cited in ibid., 181).

sist, moral judgement. But even so there is a discernible positivity about Hilla, even a love of the transformations enacted upon the landscape, the new hills and dales of the slag heaps. Hilla clearly delights in it, uplifted by the endeavour. She laughs often. She is not a pessimist. Bernd is different, however. He seems grim, actually desperate. When a plant is on the point of demolition, Bernd can get hysterical, much to Hilla's bemusement. And it is true that when these lumbering nomadic life-forms die, they leave no trace. They are quickly pulled apart, their bones picked clean and dispersed. Despite the rolling hills left in their wake, of the beasts themselves there is nothing to dig for when they are fallen.

When it was time for a break, Hilla and I left Bernd to his own devices and found a nearby hill on which to sit and talk. I picked up where we had left off at lunch and asked her how she conceived of the material she was assembling. I wanted to draw her out on the issue of typological system. It is greatly overestimated, she said, when it is admired for its own sake. She asked me to consider the strange temporality of these forms. She likened them to dragonflies that live only for a day. Life is telescoped into a few hours, the recent past is already old time, almost prehistoric. There is something 'crazy' about these architectures. They're never really finished, they're always mutating and are host to excrescences that grow upon them, odd additions grafted onto them for particular functions and to keep them up to date. They grow in this way even unto the point of collapse and death. So, while they may be functional forms, very logical and pragmatic, they have a tendency to 'craziness', to junglefication, to becoming chaos. Method is called for and typicality is the key -- ideal types...exemplary forms...Essentially, you have to cut a swathe through the jungle and identify its basic forms, she said. How do you do this? It depends on the kind of creature, the kind of design and growth you are hunting. If you are after an octopus, you need a special method to rein in its many wriggling appendages, its peculiar movements. It is the same with a blast furnace or a winding tower. This kind of photography is almost ethology or botany. It involves taming the jungle, learning its pathways, its sights, sounds and smells. I noted that at lunch we had talked mainly about death, in a kind of elegiac mode. Now we were talking about life, raw and teeming.

I confirm that this report constitutes a true and factual record.

From Hilla Becher's case notes
Mail intercept
[*The following is reproduced from tightly compacted handwriting.*]
Our investigation is making progress. We have now compiled an extensive document of evidence: winding towers, processing plants, silos, blast furnaces, lime kilns, cooling towers, water towers, gasometers.

This we have arranged in the form of typologies and comparative juxtapositions. Standing in the middle of the vast space in which the images have been arranged, grouped and labeled, Bernd and I have gazed upon the result of our years of work together: research, reconnoiters, technical precision. As Karl has so insightfully put it, this is a document of 'a second form of nature', it assembles evidence on the 'organs of technical existence.' To accomplish this, it has been necessary to maintain a rigorous systematic approach: neutrality, continuity. There can be none of the sublime associations with the power of first nature -- we have recorded the landscape without the frustrations of perspective, without the drama of cloud formations, without shadows. But this is not simply a procedure that 'shows'. Our document is one born of a refusal to be exegetical, born of a distrust of the anonymous landscape of built forms. This unremarkable background to material existence communicates something -- it represents, it reflects -- but we have refused to be complicit with this communication. We are suspicious of second nature. It is a deceptive, obfuscatory landscape. It must be confronted, decoded, unraveled. To determine the nature of this place, we have gone against its grain. We are emissaries of Hermes, wayfarers, journeying into the land.[2] Images of our travels

---

2   In the various interviews reproduced in Lange's *Bernd and Hilla Becher: Life and Work*, the Bechers describe a process that is, on one hand, interpretive and hermeneutic (Lange, for example, makes an explicit link between hermeneutics and the

surround us: Siegen, Heidelberg, Hofstede, Duisburg, Charleroi, Valenciennes, Pas-de-Calais, Cevennes, Aberdare, Pontypridd, Sheffield, Manchester, Nottingham.

[*Here follows a missing section. It appears the author has cut this from the page entirely prior to the point at which these notes came into the possession of Sektion Null. The handwritten notes then continue.*]

And yet, although we have journeyed deep into these lands, it is the surfaces that most interest us, that offer up the most clues. To gaze upon these typologies, arranged as they are, it is clear that their clues are not 'objective', not separate from the phenomenon of experience. Instead, these are concrete clues, clues rendered as forces with present intimacy, clues that bring us into a space of contact with the flesh of second nature, with the material organs of technical existence. I can feel the unhuman body of the land -- its surface -- entangled with my own surface, my skin. To gaze upon this document is to touch and be touched. Its surfaces crack, crumble and ooze, I encounter the deterioration, the decomposition, of the landscape. Faultless images transmit a strange force of life. Organs of technical existence transform and reconfigure the organ-ized body.

---

typological method, 51), and, on the other hand, phenomenological, motivated purely by description, to document without interpretation (210).

[*The next section is illegible -- the text has been obscured by scribbled occult symbols. A few lines of handwritten notes then continue on the following page, but here they appear to have been written in haste.*]

Something lives in the images. Vectors that outrun people or things. Inaccessible. It hovers. No, not IN the images, BETWEEN them, beyond them, hidden in reality's negative counterpart. In an encounter with nature as cosmic ordeal. The flesh creeps.

NONDISCLOSABLE
Seized schizoanalytic records for Becher, H.
Consultant: Dr ████████
Date: ██████
Hypnagogic therapy -- dream machine session no.5
Another fascinating session thanks to Gysin and Sommerville's extraordinary device. Despite my initial reservations, Hilla insisted upon using the machine for a period far in excess of our previous experiments. I must confess to some excitement at the thought of eventually publishing my conclusions on this ongoing series of consultations.

Hilla once again reports perceptions of the city. As before, she describes to the rest of the group images of what she insists upon calling the 'capital of the twentieth century'. Though unfamiliar to her in a normal waking state, the details of these images are remarkable. She describes a city shaken apart by its own accelerated energies. Once a place of industrial potency, it is now a drosscape, abandoned, absent of any human presence, a Zone more eerie than any of Hollywood's most prosaic visions. And yet this place is not without life. The historical centre of the city is based around a collection of grand, ornamental buildings, constructed in 'the years before the crash', as she puts it. These structures -- hotels, banks, theatres, cinemas, shopping arcades, transport terminals -- are now putrefying, their forms decomposing, inseparable from the plant matter which seems to sprout everywhere. Her tone, which is often ecstatic, suggests this is a process of revitalization rather than ruin, a renewal of the city's materiality in a form she has yet to make clear. In these images, the built landscape is itself vegetal, the forms she describes are not collapsing but mulching down.

At other times, Hilla reverts to her waking tendency toward forensic detail. She describes the decaying ballroom of a once lavish hotel, a fallen piano in a weird state of transformation, on the way to becoming some kind of fungal organism. Nearby, formerly grand residences, built in Art Deco and Spanish Revival style (such detail!), are rotting. As in her previous encounters with the dream machine, Hilla spends considerable time telling us of factories, industrial plants, and the enormous automobile works and empty assembly lines with which the rest of the group is now familiar.[3] Once again, this level of detail tests the patience of us all (though I favour this collective sense of irritability to the unease I had also begun to detect in the room).

As I bring the session to an end by turning off the machine, Hilla once again loses her grasp on the images, the city fades, it becomes indistinct, a memory.

Agent Wasserman (surveillance), shift report

[*According to an archivist's annotation, Sektion Null agent Wasserman filed these reports by Telex in the summer of 1968, shortly before his unfortunate disappearance. He was assigned to conduct Level 1 surveillance of the Bechers (during their travels in the Ruhr district??). Records indicate that Wasserman's case officer had become concerned over the tone of these reports, and a request was eventually made for Wasserman to be pulled from active duty. This request was not approved.*]

In what appears to have been a lengthy surveying process for suitable perspective, the targets spent the entire day tramping up and down the hills overlooking the plant. H & B carried a considerable amount of equipment which they hauled throughout their wanderings. During this process, their activity was continually interrupt-

---

3 In case it is not already clear, these images are inspired by the various examples of Detroit ruin porn, most notably Yves Marchand and Romain Meffre's *The Ruins of Detroit* (Göttingen: Steidl, 2010). Equally, part of this imagined description is familiar to Marchand and Meffre's study of Hashima Island, the old Mitsubishi coal mining facility.

ed by repeated discussions which, based on their gestures toward the sky, most likely concerned the light. By late afternoon, after finally setting up their equipment, it began to rain intermittently. The equipment was packed away and unpacked several times, before the targets decided to return to their Volkswagen and drive back to the hotel. No photographs were taken all day. No further activity occurred.

<u>Addendum</u>: In the evening, H & B went to the cinema where they saw FAHRSTUHL ZUM SCHAFOTT. The film tells the story of a perfect crime unraveling. In a narrative that takes place over 24 hours, the audience is presented with entangled pairs of lovers, coincidences, mix-ups, mistaken identities, fast cars, the spectre of war, murder, interrogation. Julien has killed Florence's husband and made it look like a suicide but, having forgotten to remove a piece of evidence that will tie him to the murder, he is forced to return to the scene of the crime. Once there, he becomes trapped in an elevator, the power to the building shut down overnight. Florence wanders desolately through the city at night, searching for any sign of her lover, but he seems to have disappeared. Meanwhile, Louis and Veronique have stolen Julien's car. They drive to a motel where they end up murdering a couple of German tourists -- the Benckers! Placing his car, his overcoat and his gun at the scene, the police finger Julien for the murder of this German couple. Julien's photograph appears on the front page of the

paper, a manhunt is in progress, and --
just as soon as he manages to free himself
from the elevator, he is arrested. In the
end, it is a set of photographs that sorts
out the confusion. A forgotten film from
a miniature camera, left with the motel's
processing service, puts Louis and Vero-
nique at the scene of the Benkers' murder,
just as it reveals Julien and Florence to
be lovers who conspired against her husband. The image wraps everything up, the
grizzled detective has won the day. 'Never leave photos lying around' he advises
Florence, intimating that she will face a
death sentence for her crime. The final
scene takes place in a darkroom. Latent images become visible, Miles Davis's forlorn
trumpet weeps. Florence's hands are in the
developer, fingers caressing the emulsion
of prints which show her and Julien em-
bracing, smiling. Their punishment will be
separation -- across time, across life and
death -- but they will remain together in
the image.

Note: Dr S insisted that I record any personal sensation or experience that might
be considered out of the ordinary, so here
goes. This afternoon, hidden behind a small
slag heap some distance from the targets,
I took photographs of the Bechers load-
ing their equipment back into the Volkswagen. As they prepared to leave, I quickly
headed back to my car. At this time, I became vaguely conscious of something coil-
ing around the lower part of my right leg,
but in my effort to maintain surveillance

while getting back to the car without being spotted, I simply ignored the sensation. By the time I reached the car I found there was nothing attached to my leg and assumed the plant, or whatever it was, must have snagged on something and come loose. Later, in the cinema, eight rows back from the Bechers, I became conscious of the sensation again -- an impression of something tightening on my lower leg, or what dimly felt like a vine or creeper was still wrapped around it. Even now, writing this report back at the hotel, the feeling is so distinct that I can't help but repeatedly glance down at my leg to check there is nothing entwined! I can only assume that I'm experiencing a minor allergic reaction to toxic flora, though I can't imagine how this happened -- the steel works is notable for its utter lack of vegetation.

I confirm that the foregoing is a true and accurate account.

NONDISCLOSABLE
Seized schizoanalytic records for Becher, H.
Consultant: Dr ▮▮▮▮▮▮▮▮
Date: ▮▮▮▮▮▮
Hypnagogic therapy -- dream machine session no.6
Something new... From the past we travel to the future of Hilla's fabulous city, which, in spite of her condition, is conjured with utopian vigor. After the crash, Hilla tells us with absolute confidence, the people had migrated to the flat sub-

urban areas, but even these are now without trace of the human. In the plots where abandoned houses are most decayed there are already small, dense forests. In the distance, prairie grasses. She is knotweed, a network of vines, creepers.

As she moves through the city, her descriptions become more like brief flashes: the floor of a police station littered with Polaroids, tendrils growing over, across and through the intermingled pile of suspects and victims; a clock on a high school wall, its face and hands dissolving into vegetal slime. She becomes breathless as her account of these snapshots becomes faster and faster. But as I reach to switch off the machine, she comes to a sudden halt.

The group collectively exhales as Hilla describes one final image. The city is now surrounded by photographers, every one of them a Last Man. They do not understand, she tells us in a whisper. The photographers believe it is their job to capture the triumph of Nature over human culture. For these romantic realists, the city will serve as a feature of the human landscape, as memento mori, as picturesque monument for human time.[4] It is a theme park, a Pompeii or Herculaneum for the 21st century, to be reproduced in giant limited edition tomes. But, she murmurs, the city's vegetal images are tendrillar systems, a form of media open to an immanent outside, linking

---

4   Brian Dillon, *Ruin Lust: Artist's Fascination with Ruins, from Turner to the Present Day* (London: Tate Publishing, 2014), 10.

the photographer, the human, to 'billions
of other worlds'.[5]

Agent Voss, shift report

'We are not war photographers!' Hilla insisted this afternoon when I exasperated
her with my continuing questions about
their methods. I had been very bored at
Oberhausen in the morning and had made the
mistake of betraying this to her. She explained once again why they needed to be
so well researched and prepared, so discriminating and so -- yes, let's say it,
anal -- about the way they approached the
photographs they took and their approach
to assembly and display. Emphatically, she
said, these are not sterile typologies for
the bourgeoisie to tip their wine glasses
to in their appreciation in various gallery settings. When these sequences are assembled, 'something happens'. She said it
twice, three times. Something happens, and
the best way to understand it is to conceive it as a kind of music-making. I had
heard her express this idea before and I
pressed her further. Each industrial apparatus, each object, she said, has its
own sound -- you could call it a tone or a
rhythm. It is individual, it is distinct.
It is raw sonic material, and when you ar-
range several of these forms together, you
can, with sufficient experience and skill,
cajole them into making music together. It
is a natural composition, a song of in-

---

5   Burroughs and Gysin, *The Third Mind,* 135; Michael Marder, *Plant-Thinking: A Philosophy of Vegetal Life* (New York: Columbia University Press, 2013), 42.

dustrial nature. Typological manipulation
is an orchestration of repetition, rhythm,
and the introduction of slight differences
and variations. We encounter sound in its
raw state, she said, that is, as noise. And
from it we extract *refrains*. We are agents
of the refrain. Rather grand, I commented.
But she was not to be cowed. I had touched
on something really important. She believes
that this music sounds technological nature
and that through it we can track its mu-
tations, its fluxes and congealings. This
'refraining' is an ordering of chaos, a
productivity of chaos. Hilla grew quiet at
this point. When she continued, she mumbled
some indistinct remarks on the threat posed
by 'new developments'. She connected this
to the fact that they had aborted their
plans to create typologies of radio and TV
transmitters...Before I dropped her off at
their hotel, she made some few last comments about their approach to what she said
she might call 'morphology' in preference
over typology. This approach, she insisted,
is absolutely to be conceived as occurring
in the fringes, at the edges. It is an investigation of the borderlands of twentieth-century nature -- not quite art, history or science, but something in between. As
I bid her goodnight, she reminded me that
she was deadly serious about her conten-
tion that their work was one of detection,
one of penetrating a cover-up, identifying
a crime that had been perpetrated in this
'in-between'.

I confirm that this is a true and factual record.

Extracts from Hilla Becher's case notes
Mail intercept
Reproduced from handwriting
The war between the wars.
1. Nature.
Margaret Bourke-White the herpetologist.
Friend to animals and birds, to reptiles. Walks the contours, the land, the wilderness. Lessons from the natural world.
[Illegible.]
At Columbia, she becomes a pictorialist. Soft focus. Romantic.
Machines are perceived through a humanist prism. The world is perceived by a subject.

2. Second nature. A denatured world. The geography of places. Naturalized, but socially and technically constructed.
The human is standardized, scientifically managed, exchanged and interchangeable.
Margaret Bourke-White as the spirit of the machine age.
Charles Sheeler as high priest.
The machine as cultic force, a transcendent power. Mythical.
In Cleveland and New York, Bourke-White channels a machine aesthetic. Realism and abstraction. Pattern and projection.
Henry Luce comes calling. Bourke-White and Sheeler sign up to FORTUNE. Bourke-White depicts the grandeur of industry, giant

structures. Sheeler seeks a precisionist rendering of 'Power'.[6]

To some, their work is simply homage to capital.

They monumentalize industrial forms. The power they depict is omnipotent.

There is none of Lewis Hine's humanist outrage here. Little concern for the wage labourer, for the human.

But there is something else.

Bourke-White begins to map machinic-assemblages, interrelating material objects, users and producers, new social compositions. In her work, the human is not a mere appendage to the machine, the human-machine exist in worlding relation.

Together, Bourke-White and Sheeler intimate something else, another geography of relations which extends beyond industrial territories.

This is fleeting.

After the crash, Bourke-White gives herself up to the moral humanism of LIFE. Sheeler is trapped in walled gardens of artistic expression.

But --

[*Illegible. Most of the following paragraph is heavily crossed through. Cannot be deciphered despite lab analysis. Continues with:*]

Bourke-White's photomural for RCA (1933). The broadcast sublime. The nascent network.

---

6   See Stephen Bennett Phillips, *Margaret Bourke-White: The Photography of Design 1927–1936* (The Phillips Collection, 2003); Karen Lucic, *Charles Sheeler and the Cult of the Machine* (Reaktion Books, 1991).

Sheeler's 'Self Portrait' (1923). The artist as feint [*faint?*] reflection in a pane
of glass, subjugated to the dominance of
the telephone, to the new regime of communication.

3. Telesthesia. Third nature. The present. The increasing dominance of speed over
space and place.
Second nature is encompassed by a media
layer.
Second nature is transformed. The ongoing
emanations of the crash pulse throughout
the world. Accelerating.
These processes are hidden in plain sight.
Its forms are not monumental but nomadic.

Agent Wasserman, shift report
The targets arrived back from their day's
work to their hotel at 18:00. At 18:40,
they were collected by taxi and driven to
the Restaurant Odradek. After the restaurant, they walked the several streets to
the cinema. On this occasion, the movie
they saw was a relatively new one -- an
American crime drama, *Point Blank*. The star
of the film, Lee Marvin, as 'Walker', is,
one might say, as hard as nails. In my assessment, the film envisions a new amor-
al business-type of crime and punishment
in which victims and their oppressors are
prone to switching roles in service of the
profit principle. Walker wears the mask of
affectlessness. The most obvious interpretation of the film is that Walker is living
dead, a revenant with unfinished business,
who may only act and kill indirectly, adja-

cently. But his 'revenge' ultimately enacts a peculiar complicity with the 'Organization' which it initially appears he is to bring down. The ghost becomes a puppet. Business embraces spectrality, which it remunerates in an unusual way. The most significant observation I have to make is that in this film the whole world is a set-up. Not only the actors, but also the characters they play, seem to (hesitantly) voice a pre-written script. Plus, never have I seen so many doors and windows, curtains and staircases, mirrors and other reflective surfaces in a movie. As in a theatre, where one backdrop is always ready to give way to the next, every space (and moment) harbours and is compromised by other adjacent spaces (and moments). Movement and vision is constantly impeded and subject to protocols of access, with the exception, perhaps of Walker's. Walker surfs the protocols and this is why he proves so good for business. He walks between, as it were. After the movie, I followed the targets as they returned by taxi directly to their hotel and retired at 23:30.

Later that night [*This extract is one of several assumed to have been drawn by the agent from his official dream diary, or 'noctuary'*]:
   The Captain is screaming, hands clamped around his ears. Voss's face is melting -- Jesus -- falling down his shirt in a sheet. I cannot string two thoughts together because of the immensely loud and disgusting whistling emanating from the swaying

transmitter. Moments before, the sky had grown dark, threatening storm, and then the sound had started. Bernd Becher suddenly slumped, like a wound-down automaton. I saw thick grey vines, their ends split into myriad probes, flicking around the structure's antennas, fibrillating, tasting the air. Then, Hilla is right beside me, her face inches away from mine, yelling at the top of her voice so as to be heard above the whistling transmitter: 'BRING ME IN!'

I confirm that this is a true and factual record.

Items of interest [*descriptions apparently based on observation of items found in the possession of Hilla Becher during house search*]:

A. Photograph
The somewhat grainy black and white image depicts a group of approximately 20 people. They are arranged tightly (most stand, some sit) and many faces are obscured. The majority of the group pose for the photographer, smiling, and several people clutch glasses of wine. Based on their clothing, the image was probably taken some time in the 1940s. The faces of three figures have been roughly circled in red pen: In the centre, a man dressed all in black, with black hair and thick black eyebrows; in the lower right, a woman in military uniform ignoring the camera; standing behind her, a balding man in a three piece tweed suit.

Scribbled handwriting in pencil covers the back of the photograph: Cocktails at de Brunhoff's. Capa, C-B, Miller. C-B, father of 'photojournalism', is (like Miller) disciple of surrealism. Rejects 'documenting', 'reporting'. Not interested in photojournalism label. Capa advises caution. You need an assignment or 'you'll be like a hothouse plant', he says. But in the magic of decisive moment C-B's surrealism (and his vegetal fate?) persisted. Describes particular intuition for events, fleeting chiasmas when the world extrudes a truth from its flux. Archetype probably the *flâneur,* detached city wanderer, aimless but attuned to rhythm of urban landscape. *Flâneur* picks up untimely signals: tracks lost past and anticipates impending future. C-B's images are seeing devices, not only capture eventful present but also probe its future.

B. Annotations made to working sketches
[*sketches made, it is recorded, in anticipation of a project to document British TV and radio transmitters. A field trip in the spring of '68 did take place, but plans to visit Winter Hill (Lancs), Emley Moor (Yorks) and other sites were abandoned for unspecified reasons*]
...Conundrum. Germinal ambivalence. What is it we detect, stirring in the background, infecting and disfiguring technical organs, perverting the very idea of production? Seeing that there is something that we *cannot see, throwing evidential inquiry into disarray.* Inimical, at least in-

different to our ministrations? An opacity, a phenomenon of thresholds, threatening to infect us, too. Secret devices with unrecognizable, criminal functions -- these noxious flowerings which harrow the technical body are not for us.

Agent Wasserman, shift report

The targets dined at Odradek and took in another movie. San Francisco, featured in *Point Blank,* is a weird city. It's foggy, things are blurred. Its streets rise and plunge manically. It's always on the brink of disasters -- fires, earthquakes. Vertigo, of course, is a touchstone, as is *The Maltese Falcon.* Tonight, the targets went to see Orson Welles' *The Lady from Shanghai,* which famously situates its climactic scenes in a funhouse, a hall of mirrors. Exterior shots of this building were taken at Frisco's Playland-at-the-Beach. The film presents reality as a rebus in which sense has fractured and become scattered through a process of multiple and virulent reflection. Who's aiming at who? The nightmare of mirrors demanded the studio provide nearly 3000 square feet of glass. Scenes were filmed through cleverly situated one-way mirrors. Nothing is seen straight on in this movie. Almost every line of dialogue hints at traps, framings, betrayals. 'After what I'd been through, anything crazy at all...seemed natural'. Reality is criminal through and through. Reality is reticular and murderous, like cinema itself and sense coagulates only as the network is finally destroyed by a fool.

Later [*from Wasserman's noctuary*]:
It starts in a bit of a daze. I find myself
in the Odradek at Konrad Fischer's table.
As always when I have visited this establishment, I find the ambience oddly repel-
lent. Fischer, intoxicated, is preoccupied
with trying to impress Hilla with tales of
his American artist friends. I become aware
that Bernd is photographing our group, having managed to set up his plate camera behind a nearby curtain. Hilla is very sub-
dued. Her eyes, I realize, are fixed on
mine. She slips me a napkin on which she
has scribbled a word or a sign. I discreet-
ly take it and place it upon my lap. Before
I can look at it, Fischer distracts us all
with a question: 'So who here is Sektion
Null?' It disturbs me. I am thrown into a
panic.

I confirm that this is a true and factual
record.

Agent Wasserman, shift report
Odradek and a movie. This time, Aldrich's
Kiss Me Deadly. Set in Los Angeles, the
other weird city where life is lived on a
knife's edge. Of course, commentary on this
movie is certain to revolve around the question of the 'Great Whatsit' -- the enigmatic case containing something which glows
very ominously. At the end of this movie,
what is within the case reaches critical
mass, as it inevitably must, and it makes a
chilling racket. I suppose we are all put
in mind of nuclear power. But for HB, to
paraphrase Mike Hammer, it is connected up

with something *even bigger.* I am afflicted
grievously with a migraine and, as soon as
I witness the targets go back into their
hotel, I return to my room and to bed.

Later [*noctuary*]:
I don't quite know where we are...Oberhau-
sen? Over by the blast furnaces, I seem to
see my old school. I feel certain I am late
for a lesson...My migraine has accompanied
me into the dream. It is as if the world is
cracking and splitting. HB, ignoring me, is
at work with a camera. It looks like she is
preparing to take pictures of the school.
But she walks away. When she has gone, I
wait a few moments and then approach the
large-format plate camera which, as I recall, is the pre-arranged dead drop.

Record of surveillance, Galerie Konrad Fischer

[*On the evening of Friday, January 3rd,
1969, Null agents observed events and recorded conversations on the occasion of the
opening of Robert Smithson's exhibition at
Galerie Konrad Fischer, Düsseldorf. The
targets, Hilla and Bernd Becher were in
attendance, as well as the gallery owner.
Smithson arrived fashionably late accompanied by a young artist of his acquain-
tance named Reiner Grossvogel. Smithson led
Grossvogel around the two exhibits comprising his show, which consisted of the art-
works, Nonsite (Ruhr district), five large
steel bins full of slag accompanied by wall
panels (map details, photographs, textu-
al material), and Asphalt Lump, simply a*

large, dark grey rounded lump of asphalt placed on the gallery floor, with no accompanying material. It was whilst the two were inspecting this second artwork that the first significant conversational extract was recorded as follows:]

Reiner Grossvogel: It is a rather prepossessing lump, Robert. Did you have to look for a long time to find it? Refined bitumen from Oberhausen?

Robert Smithson: No, it was just lying there. I liked this particular dollop. You know, it never fully solidifies, it's always mid-flow, trapping and corrupting everything that touches it. In its natural form, it trapped the mammoths -- in the tar pits, you know? The first photographs were made using asphalt-coated plates...I'm interested in thinking in lumps, piles, heaps. We would do well to think like matter -- do you know the old alchemical maxim, *solve et coagula*? The world reduced to processes of dissolution and coagulation. All architectures ooze away or turn to stone, even the architecture of the self, the soul. Becoming turbid, foggy and confused.

RG: Photography and tar? That's interesting. Somehow primordial, this technology, isn't it?

RS: I imagine technologies being pulled into the pit, overwhelmed. Or, alternatively, think of the most advanced technologies as animal or insect. Just ripping, biting,

95

burrowing, fucking. I dream of a world of non-containment. These non-sites are really bits broken off of chaos, tentacles from the abyss. If we can *contain the non-contained,* however briefly, map it, well...we need a good dose of it, is all I'm saying.

[*At this point, Smithson and Grossvogel move on to the Non-site (Ruhr district) exhibit, where they join Hilla Becher and Konrad Fischer. After introductions and several minutes of pleasantries, the following extract was recorded:*]

RS: We both want to crack the case, Hilla, but with me -- as I was just telling Reiner -- it's literal. I want to create fissures in containers, open them up to their internal caverns. With me it's about applying friction, which is also a matter of fiction. If there has been a crime, I'm seduced by the villain. If this is an aftermath, I think maybe there's something in the ensuing alarm to celebrate. The collapse of order, it's a peculiar kind of illumination, like peeling off a rind or crust, or turning rocks over and watching the teeming life racing for darkness.

Hilla Becher: You're incorrigible! If this is a crime, how will you make the charges stick?!

RS: It will never reach trial, Hilla. It's not Sherlock Holmes. It's more like the hardboiled stuff...*film noir*...with truth running scared like those insects, everybody compromised. This is a crime that sends us all scuttling.

Konrad Fischer: It's not just a crime. It's a crimewave!

RS: Precisely. It's a necessary evil -- this gallery, these fences we put up around everything...no offence, Konrad...but these non-sites of mine I see as kind of guiltless because they are as much outside the room as inside. They are elsewhere, mapping the entrance to the abyss. They are where the 'garden' runs riot, grows extravagantly and weirdly, so to speak. My job as an artist is to make the landscape reel, make the garden tumultuous and voracious.

[*The last extract of conversation was recorded towards the close of the evening, after the aforementioned have sought refreshment in a nearby bar. Smithson waxes lyrical on one of his key influences:*]

RS: Hilla, do you know of T.E. Hulmes's work...an art critic, turn of the century? No? He wrote a marvellous essay, called 'Cinders', which I think of often. Hulme says reality is 'cindery' in nature -- cinders are pyroclastic rocks, full of cavities, formed in volcanic action. So, reality is the temporary coagulation, cooling down, of exploded matter. It's thrown out and it forms where it lands. Hulme associates cinders with the 'fringe' of things. He says, and I can quote this verbatim: 'Always think of the fringe and of the cold walks, of the lines that lead nowhere'. And again: 'Great men, go to the outside, away from the Room, and wrestle with the cinders. And cinders become the Azores, the Magic Isles'. The cinders are a source of friction, an incitement to those who refuse to leave the Room...[7]

HB: When we were at Oberhausen, you were so casual, even careless. No regard for the weather, the light, anything. I thought you were making it up as you went along. Just snapping away! Bernd was so dismayed! Now, I think you are the *Cinderman*. I think you are not human! [*Laughter*]

Letters regarding Smithson in Yucatán
i) Entropological Drift
[*It is believed that these fragments derive from letters sent to H.B. by Reiner Grossvogel in spring '69 and relate to Smithson's trip to Yucatán during which time Smithson 'channelled' what is here referred to as the 'intersection mythos'.*]

El hombre's tendrils are all over this. This drug -- the brujos extract it from the crushed or scraped bark of some vine -- opens a fellow up to 'insane overwhelming rape of the senses...Everything stirs with a peculiar furtive writhing life like a Van Gogh painting...There is a definite sense

---

7   T.E. Hulme, 'Cinders', in *Speculations: Essays on Humanism and the Philosophy of Art*, ed. Herbert Read (London: Kegan Paul, Trench, Trubner & Co., 1936), 215–45.

of space time travel...'[8] Coupled with the 'mirror-travel' trick -- ever since New York, elsewhere, and all the time on this trip -- this is potent magic. And it's connected to the plant thing. I call to your attention Burroughs's 'autobiography': 'I have no past life at all being a notorious plant or "intrusion" if you prefer the archaeological word for an "intruded" artifact...Remember? I prefer not to'.[9] This trick is a way *back* 'outside', *extrusion* through the mirror. 'Straight exploration', Burroughs says -- mainlining the intersection mythos. Bluntly: on this 'anti-expedition', RS has made himself into a channel, a medium.

A couple of pointers: ONE -- The reading material he devoured in preparation. Two books in particular: James Churchward's *The Lost Continent of Mu* and Peter Nehemkis's *Latin America: Myth and Reality*.[10] Churchward was an occult writer (big favourite of Lovecraft) who theorized that the continent of Mu, under the Pacific Ocean, was the Garden of Eden (*Garden*, see) and roped this together with a ton of ancient

---

8   William S. Burroughs, 'Letter to Allen Ginsberg, July 8, 1953', in William S. Burroughs: Letters 1945-59, ed. Oliver Harris (London: Penguin Classics, 2009), 180.

9   William S. Burroughs, 'Letter to Allen Ginsberg, October 27, 1959', in *William S. Burroughs: Letters 1945--9*, ed. Oliver Harris (London: Penguin Classics, 2009), 433.

10 Much of this detail is taken from Ann Reynolds, *Robert Smithson: Learning from New Jersey and Elsewhere* (Cambridge, MA: MIT Press, 2003). See, in particular, chapter 3. See also Smithson's own account, 'Incidents of Mirror-Travel in the Yucatán', in *Robert Smithson: The Collected Writings*, ed. Jack Flam (Berkeley: University of California Press, 1996 [1969]), 119--33. Simon O'Sullivan's discussion of the Mirror Displacements is also useful: Simon O'Sullivan, *Art Encounters Deleuze and Guattari: Thought Beyond Representation* (Houndmills: Palgrave Macmillan, 2006), 105--10.

mythology. The Nehemkis volume is an altogether more sober affair. The Churchward is grubby, well-thumbed, while the Nehemkis is barely touched, spine not even cracked. TWO -- RS rents a car, jumps in with NH and VD and tears down highway 261, eventually hitting Palenque (Chiapas). Along the way, frequent stop-offs at various Mayan ruins. These times, he drags out the mirrors and arranges them very particularly, pushed into the earth or lodged amongst roots and vines. Out comes the Instamatic. The mirrors displace everything they reflect, intersecting and calling forth virtualities, cicerones in the form of Mayan and Aztec Gods. So they speak to him, phrases such as: 'The true fiction eradicates the false reality'. And then it's all dismantled and nothing left but the pictures.

Alien crash sites, traces of an *entropological* drift to unhuman time, these sites are death knells, haecceities which plug into other dimensions. Mirrors cracking, ravines in an insect's carapace. (Not) here and (not) now.

Agent Wasserman, shift report
Rained all day. No activity.

Note: I must record a further development to the sensation described in my previous personal report. This morning, as has become my habit during the Bechers' stay at this hotel, I went to the café across the street for breakfast. The establishment is ideally situated to allow continuous observation of the targets' Volkswagen, and the waitress has recognized my preference for a table by the window. Today, though, as she was showing me to the table, the waitress quietly warned me of the café's hygiene policy. I really shouldn't come into the establishment, she whispered, with all those weeds trailing from my legs like that. Perhaps next time I could make sure I have cleaned myself up a bit. She was sure I'd understand -- it's not fair on the other customers, after all. Well, I was shocked. But surely this can only be coincidence? Even though, before she had even stopped speaking, it was clear that there was -- of course -- nothing tangled around my legs, the waitress insisted on retracing our journey from the entrance, and checking under other tables, in the expectation of finding some knot of vines or creepers caught on café furniture. Needless to say, the incident was embarrassing for both of us, and I will not return to the café again.

This is true and factual.

Agent Wasserman, shift report
Bright sunshine. The light appears to be too harsh for the images of the water tower the Bechers had planned to capture today. They sit in the Volkswagen for several hours, waiting, I assume, for a change to the light, but eventually they give up. Instead, they drive to the office of a local mining company, where they meet with the manager. My interrogation of the manager (conducted later in the evening) reveals that, despite his suspicions of their mo-

tives, he was willing to provide them with maps, schematics, and various other files relating to the company's activities in the area.

Note: Tonight, making my way back to the hotel after interrogating the manager of the mining company, I saw some kind of weeds growing up out of the street.

I confirm...There is no doubt this time, they were emerging from the concrete in front of my eyes, following me as I moved along the pavement...

Letters regarding Smithson in Yucatán
ii) Smoke

...the mind's secret mindlessness. The mind is like mud, or slime. That's the general idea. Moved by a force -- a chaos, an infection maybe, something called *the Tsalal*.[11] A sculpting, shaping force that vitalizes everything, alive or dead, organic or inorganic, pushing things apart, eroding and rotting them, and pulling them together, gluing them. Think of any number of processes: putrefaction, or rusting, corrosion, or the action of an earthquake or a geyser, a landslide or a flood. All of

---

11   Sources here again include Smithson's 'Incidents of Mirror-Travel in Yucatán', but also Thomas Ligotti's short story, 'The Shadow, The Darkness', in *Teatro Gottesco* (London: Virgin, 2008), 243–80. Ligotti's *Tsalal* is inspired by the name of an island in Edgar Allan Poe's *The Narrative of Arthur Gordon Pym of Nantucket* (1838). Poe took it from the Hebrew, in which it refers to endarkenment and, also, to cover, to sink into, and to vibrate with fear. Poe's *Tsalal* is located within the Antarctic Circle, close to the abyssal vortex which he, it is thought, imagined to comprise the pole itself.

these and more...the experiment proves that this... force... can be *embraced* by any willing medium...collusion with the metamorphic designs of *the Tsalal.* Bob's insisting that this thing -- it's everything, things when they're not fenced in -- voices itself through local Gods. Gods spoke through the air-conditioner of the rental car, through the wind whistling around the car, wind through trees and over bushes, in the tide, in crumbling earth and tumbling rocks, in the click and wind of his Instamatic, in radio interference. As Smoke, it caught his eye in the rear-view mirror and told him to throw away his guide books. It's an art of wandering and it's your feet that see the way. Hands that dig without knowing what they'll touch. Abasement of vision, 'negative seeing'. Smoke said vision must be made to crawl. The further he went down the highway, the more intense this riff about the falsehood of nature, that nature is a disguise or cover-up which can be made to drop, and that Smoke's art *is* this dismantling. Nowhere places, places of dirt, ash, mud -- like a charred field, a stretch of desert, jungle. Horrible places, sometimes. At Palenque, in the jungle, his mirrors reflected the tentacular contortions of the trees, snarling vision up in sacred networks, zones of indecision and indeterminacy. Sight mutated into 'knotted reflection'. Turning over rocks, photographing the tracks of insects and animal burrows -- 'gateways to the abyss', Bob said -- and muttering about animals and insects having their own art, installed in 'a damp cosmos of fungus and mold'. A tree planted upside down becomes 'a giant vegetable squid'. Introducing friction into a fenced-in world, rubbing things up against each other, the idea being to make them travel. Travel *backwards,* he said, but a new backwards, 'over the unfathomable'.

Fragment of intercepted letter from HB, Spring 1969, to unknown:
They say they protect the constitution but are themselves overwhelmed by the scale of that which is emerging. They are intoxicated with it and elect themselves as brokers of the shadows. If it was only a few spies against us, I would not care. I have endured worse in my life. But what if we are not masters even of ourselves? I think, sometimes, my own words merely echo its whispers. Worse -- it takes my work and makes it mute. For all of these paranoid forensics on which Bernd and I have laboured, I fear it cannot be revealed in its very structure. It is nothing that will be positively detected. Nothing that will ever pause for our cameras. I believe it is alive, but I do not believe it can be known. The secret we look for has perhaps today become the 'constitution' itself.

NONDISCLOSABLE
Seized schizoanalytic records for Becher, H.
Consultant: Dr ▮▮▮▮▮▮▮
Date: ▮▮▮▮▮
Hypnagogic therapy -- dream machine session no.8

At the beginning of group discussion, Hilla refers to these sessions as part of her investigative or archaeological process. This process, she announces rather obliquely, is as much about negative evidence -- a 'gulf', a 'limit point', a 'void' -- as it is about detection or discovery. As the group's recent experience suggests, a confrontation with this paradox is fundamental, even if it takes a toll in other ways. Like any other kind of archaeology, it is a process that can't be reversed -- by which I mean that Hilla's perception of the world, her belief in the world -- has been irrevocably transformed. She appears to be cultivating an almost mystical state of consciousness.

As with the sessions of previous days, today Hilla again reports perceptions of industrial forms. She begins by describing a blast furnace, a structure which 'corresponds to a skinless body.' Over 25 minutes, we hear of its complex tangle of pipes trapping gases and directing them toward purification and processing, we hear of its cooling system of ducts and boxes, we are made to picture in detail its steel shell, its shaft, its cone. She describes these images calmly and at length before falling silent.

Though she remains positioned in front of the machine, her eyes still closed, she does not speak. After a minute or two, I assume she has simply fallen asleep. Perhaps the sheer unremitting detail of the image has exhausted her (I must confess to fighting the weight of my own eyelids at one stage during this session). But as I move across the room to gently rouse her, she abruptly resumes her description.

This time, though, nothing is clear. We have evidently moved to encounter a different form, but Hilla finds herself incapable of describing it. Eventually, amidst a series of discomforted noises, she mumbles that it is a 'box', dark and indistinct. Is this a new encounter, I ask, is this a new form? 'You mean progress,' she snaps back. 'Past to present to future. Of course not. No, not new, something old. Ancient. After the future.' Silence again. And then, just as in session no.6, she addresses Max, her son. Max is drawing the structure in crayon, an image that reminds her of something she has seen before. But the drawing is just grey, she says -- to him or to us, I'm not sure -- a grey print, flatter than the sky, formless.

2.3 | I am Muybridge

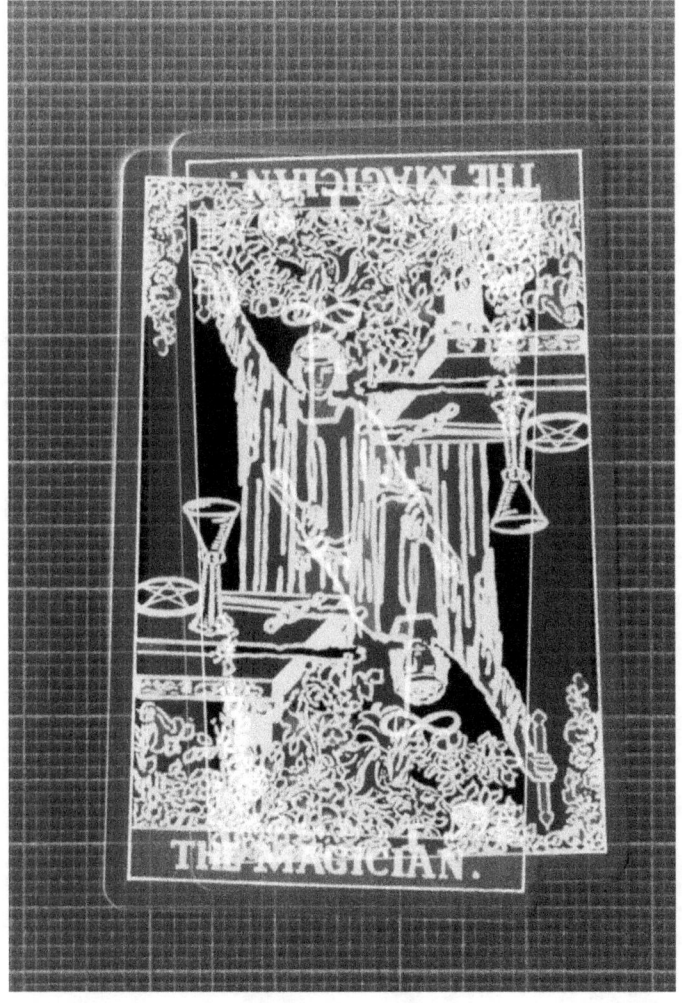

Eadweard Muybridge retired to Kingston-upon-Thames in his native England at the age of 67, giving sporadic talks and lectures but no longer involved in photographic experimentation. What we believe to be his last public appearance, a lecture to the Society for Ontofabulatory Research, took place on 15th October 1897. This event occurred during a busy period for Muybridge as he prepared the publication of two books, Animals in Motion *and* The Human Figure in Motion. *Yet, for whatever reason, the lecture has been virtually expunged from official histories. Thankfully details of his talk are preserved in a series of notes and impressions taken by members of the audience and since collected by Society archivists. The accounts concur that the auditorium chosen for the lecture, which offered seating for 300, in fact played host to an audience of almost double this number, on what was an unseasonably warm evening. It is notable, however, that the accounts of the lecture itself — excerpts of which follow below — prove to be somewhat contradictory.*

LETTER from A.H. to Phoebe Green

Dearest Phoebe,

I promised to write and here it is, but I shall be brief as I am weary from the events of the day. I was press-ganged, you see, into attending Muybridge's lecture for your brother's Society. Muybridge, that's right — still standing and still as downright peculiar! The strangest lecture it was … much of it has receded into fog already, though it concluded but a couple of hours ago. I sat next to a delightful woman, Miss Alice Johnson. She is in her thirties, I would say, and quite a prominent member of that other lot, the Society for Psychical Research. She is Mrs. Sidgwick's secretary, don't you know, and co-authored her Report on the Census of Hallucinations a while back. Do you recall it? How many sane and decent members of the British public have experienced waking hallucinations? Answer: 10 percent. Startlingly, many of these events are reported to coincide quite exactly with accidents, deaths and so on. The one who suffered the accident appears and speaks to the poor soul afflicted with the phenomenon. Alice was also involved in the mysterious Eastbourne experiments and tells me she was the first to spot so-called 'cross-correspondences' (that is, when the same phrases, images and puzzles occur to several different mediums simultaneously — spreads like a virus, she led me to believe). You might ask why she might find diversion in Muybridge's routine, but she was, in fact, director of the Balfour Biological Laboratory for Women at Cambridge for a few years and has an acute interest in animal morphology. In fact, there's more to it, I suspect. Muybridge's lecture took an odd turn into waters much closer to her more recent concerns. It seems to me, now that I mention it, that a lot of what Muybridge was venturing actually tied up with topics psychical. Alice was most animated to see his new slides… Personally, I regret the absence of the moving pictures, though they really are ten a penny these days, I suppose. Guess who Alice came with? One was that Mudge fellow, Eyeless Bill (he disturbs me, I must confess). The other was the Frenchman, Bergson! More later, Phoebe, for I cannot keep my eyes open. I must sleep. I hope I will not dream of those last slides Muybridge showed us…

Till tomorrow…

LECTURE NOTES of Miss Pamela Coleman Smith

We have been sun worshippers, knowing him as the great god Helios, as he who drives his shining chariot across the earth. Tonight he reveals himself as Charon, ferryman of Hades, the son of an unholy union between darkness and the night. His filthy form — magnificently repulsive, gloriously terrifying! — materializes before us, a cloudy matted beard hanging from his chin, a bedraggled cloak suspended from his shoulders, a crooked staff in his firm hand. He is ancient now, but possesses a dark vitality. And his eyes! Those eyes burned in their sockets and I knew I should not dare meet them, yet I could not resist. The particulars of his talk are lost to me. I remember only an image, a dim lantern slide glowing weakly in the cavernous auditorium: a dark mass of trees somewhere in California's Yosemite Valley, white mountains in the background. A blasted tree curves its way up the left hand side of the frame and a black river cuts through the land. Styx! It is here, in these dismal waters, that he reigns. Other gods fear this middleness but its harsh flows render him invulnerable, invincible. In the image, he stands at the edge of a wooden frame that extends from the Stygian banks of horror. The lone crew of his vessel, he grips an oar with which he might steer a path through the void. He is conveyor, a link, a mediator of time and space, of trajectories of existence. He exists in the middle, in a threshold that remains immanent to itself. He connects us to that which remains inaccessible.[1]

LECTURE NOTES of Mr Frederick Flash

Mister Muybridge, Helios, the old photographer, strode in precisely on time, trailing a faint chemical scent behind him, and looking older and more haggard than his years. His visage was positively mage like, his jagged white beard set against the dark tone of his overcoat (which, even in warmth of the evening, he chose not remove), his deep set, intense eyes darted about the rapt audience. In spite of appearances, though, he is energetic, fit. He paces as he talks, continuously. And in spite of his frankly rather odd accent, he commands attention. Initially, though, he appeared somewhat bored by his own material.

In his introduction, the Society's chair had attempted to offer an interpretation of Muybridge's images as scientific portraits, mechanisms for newly recognizing and comprehending subjects, identities, and bodies. He told us that they expressed universal properties, an essential humanity through which we might reconsider our selves as individuals in our differences and sameness. He did not get far with this introduction before Muybridge brusquely waved him aside and launched into a perfunctory presentation aimed at explicating his electro-photographic investigation of consecutive phases of muscular actions. On this evening he chose to dispense entirely with the Zoopraxiscope in favour of lantern slides, explaining that he wished to show sequences as individual images and as a grid. Photographic images, he explained, are not simply *of* something, they *do* something, they have a function. And so, 10ft high on the auditorium wall, we were shown gridded (and, I must admit, rather titillating) images of athletic men and ethereal women. The activities of the nude or slightly draped men were often productive — bricklaying, blacksmithing, shoveling, heaving boulders — while the activities of nude

---

1   Virgil, *The Aeneid* (London: Penguin, 2003), 121–22; Philip Brookman, *Eadweard Muybridge* (London: Tate Publishing, 2010). The image to which Smith refers is Muybridge's *Charon at the Ferry* (21), 1867, originally presented as two albumen silver prints on studio card.

or diaphanously draped women were less easy to define — skipping, dancing a pirouette, walking and flirting a fan, pouring water, getting into bed, turning around in surprise and running away, carrying a cup of tea. Though Muybridge announced these images clearly and referred carefully to their various features without hesitation, it was clear that his mind was elsewhere. He ignored two fawning questions from the floor and, at one point losing his train of thought entirely, muttered bitterly about the loss of many of his images to a warehouse fire.

Of course, that our speaker for the evening was something of an eccentric hardly proves to be an uncommon trait in those that have stood before the collected members of the Society. Nor is his eccentricity especially surprising in this instance, given the somewhat infamous events of his past and the well publicized images of his risk taking ventures. However, Mister Muybridge seemed to cultivate a strange physical relation to his photographic material. As he spoke, he frequently wandered into the beam of the projected lantern slide, pausing in the centre and causing the photographed images to overlay his own body. It was almost as if he knew that his face was overlaid with facial images — faces of so many stern athletes, so many vacant ladies. On one occasion the effect was genuinely unsettling, though difficult to describe — for a brief moment what I saw appeared to be not simply the image of one head projected on top of another but Muybridge's own head transformed, dismantled, its heretofore imperceptible qualities … released.

It was, though, only when he began presenting images that were aberrations from the ideal, or tended more toward the grotesque — contortionists, amputees, the obese — that his mood shifted. The duration for which each image was displayed notably decreased, the velocity of the evening seemed to accelerate. His eyebrows twitched, he gesticulated more wildly. The body is 'overcoded', he told us, its deviance from patterns of conformity is restricted. In his photographs the grids appear to stand in for these patterns, for machines which restrict and delimit bodily perception of the world. The grids reveal that these mechanisms do not simply stop at the body itself but extend into the landscape, into a predefined, pre-photographed world in which the body operates. This, he insisted, means that a portrait of the human cannot be restricted to the human. It must also seek to express the human's 'incompleteness', its entanglements (by this point there were murmurs of confusion, perhaps incredulity, from certain sections of the audience).[2]

If the majority of the lecture took the form of a tired performance, its finale was pure phantasmagoria. Here, Muybridge was fully animated, summoning the audience to a hush. Without fanfare, he introduced work that had never been shown before — indeed, before this evening it was generally thought that he had retired from photographic experimentation altogether. But here he revealed a bizarre late turn in his work. There can scarcely have been an individual in the auditorium unaware of Muybridge's near death experience as a passenger on that ill-fated mail coach. And it is unthinkable that anyone would have anticipated his strange response to that crash, his recreation. I can but describe the images. From the way it was arranged, the coach appeared to have swerved violently, tipped over, and sustained considerable damage. Here, though, Muybridge and his group of assistants had not staged the crash in San Francisco or some other part of the 'wild west', but in what he announced as Kingston upon Thames high street. Some of the images set the action against a familiar grid, but in others the grid was absent and the mundane goings on of Kingston life interrupted Muybridge's conventional scientific aesthetic. A number of bemused spectators were shown crowding around the crash site — a woman smoking, a police officer, a child with a balloon and ice cream gawping at the broken vehicle. A butchers shop and ophthalmic opticians could be seen in the background. Surprisingly, for an imaging technician so associated with precision, these images were poorly exposed, their details were imprecise, not quite clear. More shocking is that, a few feet in front of the wreckage, and barely perceptible in a portion of the image rendered almost entirely white, lay the naked figure of Muybridge himself, contorted on the cobbles, his luminous body entangled with remnants of a buckled wheel, parts of a door wrenched off its hinges, and the twisted figure of a horse, all four of its hooves lifted off the ground. The pro-

---

2   See plateau 7 of Deleuze and Guattari's *A Thousand Plateaus*.

jected image of Muybridge showed a face at once vividly contorted in pain and radiantly ecstatic. Helios.

The wizard standing before us jabbed at his clicker so quickly that the projectionist could not keep up. At the time it seemed to me (and, I would wager, to the rest of the audience) that this series of images had more resemblance to tableaux vivant than consecutive phases of a single occurrence, and yet the images also resonated with the power of a crash — with the force of impact, with the demolition of solidity — more so than the flickering images of a zoopraxiscope, more so than the cinematographic images made by those otherwise brilliant Frenchmen. As he moved to a second series, I was briefly overcome with a sort of waking concussion — double vision, a loss of taste, loss of smell. Here, in a similarly overexposed portion of the image Muybridge's assistants (also naked) were shown lifting his body — his *bodies* — from the wreckage and placing him onto a stretcher, their movements and gestures formally recorded in a sequence as apparently banal as that of the woman walking, turning and ascending stairs we saw earlier this evening. Now, though, it seems clear that phases occurring in the act of turning around — turning, probing — can operate against the exigencies of the present, can invoke nonhuman temporalities, can photograph the so-called future, can accelerate the dismantling of the face, of the body, before the shutter clicks. It's an old photographer's trick.[3]

FROM THE MAGICAL DIARY of Mr Conrad Paxton[4]

This evening, I attended, as honoured guest, the great Stretcher's lecture to the Society of Ontofabulatory Research. Helios! This Giant, like the first Titans, has fallen and here he announced it! He distanc-

3 'There was a small wound on the top of my head. When I recovered each eye formed an individual impression, so that, looking at you, for instance, I could see another man sitting by your side. I had no taste nor smell, and was very deaf. These symptoms continued in an acute form for probably three months. I was under medical treatment for over a year.' Muybridge, cited in Brian Clegg, *The Man Who Stopped Time: The Illuminating Story of Eadweard Muybridge — Pioneer Photographer, Father of the Motion Picture, Murderer* (Joseph Henry Press, 2007), 26–27.

4 For more on Conrad Paxton, see Laird Barron's 'Hand of Glory', in *The Beautiful Thing That Awaits Us All and Other Stories* (San Francisco: Night Shade Books, 2013).

es himself from his moving pictures at precisely the moment they are seized and championed by the new immortals, the upstart Gods of Olympian filmed entertainment! An awful Titanomachy has already been fought and lost — I fathom the enciphered meaning of those final most splendid pictures of the coach accident. Yet still, he lives and is truly immortal! And there is yet an energy and an invention which he is compelled to pour forth, a last flourish before a long and necessary silence. The Titan, the Shaman, presents, in compendium, the work of a lifetime because he is mindful of the question of legacy. The body — his body — is removed from the catastrophe to be embalmed, preserved and packaged for its future transmission. Tonight, though, we witnessed plural bodies. Just so, there are, of course, plural legacies. There are legacies for the masses and legacies for the Initiated. We, the Initiated, know that, as operations of the Son of Ouranos, God of Magic, the Titan's studies in motion are barbarous evocations of forces with multifarious applications. They side-step the rational and the conscious, tunneling holes in the wake world. The numbered gridding of humans and animals, frozen in time and space, only stands in for (and distracts the unwary observer from) a more subtle web, spun to detain and harness forces more profound, more mutative and acrobatical than the arithmetic powers of mere calculation and accumulation.

There is much he has not shown. Helios plans to bequeath most generously of his work and inventions to the good people of Kingston. But the other bequest — those unseen materials — will comprise his gift to me. The iceberg beneath the tip. Helios titillates the masses with — for example — his composition of the weird sisters brandishing their broomsticks by the emissions of the fumaroles of San Francisco's Geyser Canyon (to say nothing of the devils and glyphs scratched onto various negatives already exposed to the public domain), but of the weirdness that came after, all is shrouded. This is merely a crumb of the riches promised in the shadow bequest. Moreover, he has spoken to me — in extension of this bequest — of his plans, projects to conclude his life's experiment, and here I divulge these in this magical record.

Project the First: Insect Events. Helios proposes a further and final battery of motion studies which shall engineer sequences of images of the movements and gestural life of insects. Ostensibly, as a pragmatic matter of attracting funding, this is in furtherance of the dream of human flight. There shall be the moments of flight in winged insects — flies, dragonflies, butterflies and moths and so forth. However, away from the light, there shall also be studies of the vibratory dimension of insect life, of the action of the stridulatory organs of the crickets, grasshoppers and various beetles. There shall, of course, also be wriggly worms and undulating serpents. But further on, and deeper, there shall be studies of the motion of other, less prosaic Animalia. Nothing that walks upon the earth, but rather things that crawl, slither, slide, totter, twist, squirm and giggle in ways scarcely conspicuous in the world we know.

Project the Second: Helios ushered me into his rooms to proudly present the Book that he has begun. It is a book of scraps, an assemblage of press clippings, reports, images, assorted dispatches and documentary materials which he has amassed over the course of his career. I called it his Book of Vectors, and he approved. The Book constitutes an exploded view of my Father's genius. But it is many things — an illustration of components, a fabulation of a life, an authentic grimoire designed to conjure time and space, to tip them off their rails and catch and ride them as they propel all things into unknown infinity.[5] This is a Book that gives the world a different origin and a different cause. It is a Book that will make things happen. Here will ultimately be a diagram of technical-magical practice that Helios envisages will shatter the modern world, the world of mundane industry. Behind the sensory affordances made possible by industrialized nature, industrialized time and space, is another realm, born of a third nature, time and space in triplicate (and more). This is the secret of my Father's life and work. His whole endeavor has been a magic of movement, force and vector. Far from merely establishing an art of conjuring movement of pictures, he has achieved access to

---

5   Muybridge's Scrapbook, begun in 1894 but worked on in earnest from 1897, is the focus of Stephen Barber's *Muybridge: The Eye in Motion* (Chicago: Solar Books, 2012), in which the book is described as an 'anti-temporal grimoire'. Barber also discusses the 'myth' of Muybridge's garden-simulacrum of the Great Lakes.

another, more chaotic and diabolical, movement beyond picture.[6] A portraiture of vectors and bodies in motion rather than the banality of the frontally posed human face (from which Helios has unremittingly swerved all his career). This is the true meaning of Helios' Flying Studio! Flight from the mundane into and upon the winds blowing through other dimensions of reality. Inconspicuous powers brewing in the spaces between the things we can ordinarily see.

Project the Third: The Titan's Garden. The Book complete, my Father's final role will be gardener of a fantastical variety. It will involve strenuous labour but he is determined it shall, from start to finish, be solely the work of his own muscle and sinew. He has schooled himself in the Theory of Gardens, beginning with Cicero's De Nature Deorum (Of the Nature of the Gods) and plowing through a number of Renaissance authorities.[7] In Cicero's scheme, the sowing of crops, forestry and invention of irrigation techniques are all considered to constitute the creation of a second nature within the first nature of the Gods. This is the landscape of human infrastructures. Renaissance writers, going further than Cicero, proposed the idea of *terza natura,* a third nature proper to the project of the garden. To garden, as it is held by the Initiated, is to practice an occult art, to draw out the fantastical and the weird within the natural, to marshall and fashion the action of nonhuman forces in service of the glory of Initiates. To garden is to evoke the power of the weed, of fruiting, fungal bodies, as much as flower, grass and tree. For the satisfaction of the uninitiated, Helios plans to reconfigure his garden as an exact scale model of the Great Lakes of North America, but the true core of the project will comprise the interment of a germinative machine. My Father plans to bury a homunculus of himself…

LECTURE NOTES of Prof. William James

He spoke of images ostensibly presented to us on lantern slide, but they were images perceptible only to the man himself — to my eyes

---

6 In *The Vorrh* (Croydon: Honest Publishing, 2007), B. Catling imagines Muybridge's art and science to involve the search for a 'causeway around picture'.

7 See the chapter, 'The Idea of a Garden and the Three Natures', in John Dixon Hunt's *Greater Perfections: On the Practice of Garden Theory* (Philadelphia: University of Pennsylvania, 2000).

the projection screen simply throbbed with a prickly light, I could detect no form within its intense field no matter how convincingly Muybridge fired his clicker. Indeed, I cannot express what I saw tonight by using words I would normally call upon to describe visual phenomena. For the duration of Muybridge's talk, the entire auditorium was bathed in pure light. After he had been speaking for perhaps twenty minutes, my vision simply extinguished, I no longer found it possible to sense whether my own eyes were closed or open.[8] To me, it seemed that Muybridge's voice had enveloped the room, it came from everywhere, and it was clear that I was not the only one experiencing such symptoms. Amidst a succession of startled shuffling, low moans and occasional gasps from the audience, his voice announced that the indiscernible images had been selected from two sets. The first was produced half way across America, during a journey from north Texas to an army infirmary at Fort Smith. The second was produced in Napa County jail.

Of the first, Muybridge described images that claim to show the lower Cross Timbers, a narrow stretch of ancient woodland — in places not fifteen miles wide — cutting off direct communication between the interior prairies and the grasslands of the Great Plains. He spoke at length about this dense, deciduous zone, about this slim thicket of oaks. Inadequate for farming, unsuitable for lumber production and unfriendly to travellers, the terrain has so far remained imperceptible to the human desire for built forms, to the production of second nature. It remains a middle ground, he told us, a hiding place for packs of animals, a space used by native Indians in which to move undetected. But as an unconscious survivor of the Butterfield Overland Stage, Muybridge himself had journeyed undetected through this space.[9] In the middle, he had disappeared, he had be-

---

8   Brian Massumi, *Parables of the Virtual: Movement, Affect, Sensation* (Durham and London: Duke University Press, 2002), 145.

9   We estimate that Muybridge's unconscious journey would have taken him from north Texas (some sources state that the accident occurred north of Fort Worth, others suggest it occurred somewhere near the Brazos river) through Oklahoma and just over the border to Fort Smith in Arkansas. In Muybridge's own account, he says that upon coming to at Fort Smith, he found himself 180 miles away from the site of the coach accident. This would probably place the incident somewhere

come a movement, he had dissolved, merged with the forces that surrounded him. It was in this chaosmosis, he recounted, that his present became overwhelmed by future potentials. It was here that his desire to transform the present according to such futures took hold and started to accelerate.

He told us of his reawakening at Fort Smith. Coming to in an infirmary bed, he felt himself poised between the no longer and the not-yet. Days after the crash, after his damaged body had been transported nearly two-hundred miles north, after he had first regained consciousness, the 'arrangement' of life was different to before. He had lost himself — his self (and I can only say that I believe I experienced something similar in the auditorium tonight). Life, for Muybridge, is now mobile, multiple, it no longer bears his name. His characteristic refrains — 'I am Muybridge', 'My name is Muybridge' — are at once points of order amidst this turmoil and expressions of its instability, of the fracturing of everything circumscribed by such refrains, statements of his nonexistence in any recognizable form. And yet, this sorcerer that stood somewhere before us was able to conjure with life's multiplicity, to perform tricks with it. The images he presented to us this evening can be seen only in the periphery, by seeing beyond what can be seen, as one might imagine a conjurer to see. For a moment, I believe I glimpsed such images, magnifications of something secret, images that catch life in the middle, spectrally.

Finally, the voice that was at once a cloak and a flock, told us of the second set of images, the examples of which were again elusive, awash in a field of vivid brilliance. He claims they were produced in a cell at Napa County jail, in a space suspended between death and life, a space in which all possibilities existed, in which nothing was excluded except stability. It was written correspondence between his wife and Major Harry Larkyns that had communicated their affair, and Muybridge had travelled to Yellow Jacket Mine late at night in

---

in the south east part of lower Cross Timbers. The dendrological information on this area is courtesy of The Ancient Cross Timbers Consortium (hosted by the University of Arkansas Tree-Ring Laboratory), available at http://www.uark.edu/misc/xtimber.

order to deliver his own reply. From his cell, he had visualized the moment when Larkyns had come to the doorway. The Major had looked out into the porch, but he could see only darkness, a void. This was not an absence, Muybridge seemed to whisper in my ear, but a totality. He had grown to become imperceptible, the space he inhabited was not phenomenal but abstract.

By the time my vision had returned to its normal state, the arc lamp had long since died, and there was no sign of Muybridge.

FROM THE PHONOGRAPH DIARY of Dr E. Dunning (transcript)
I make this brief recording immediately upon my return from a most bizarre evening in the company of 'Professor' Muybridge. I had attended this occasion as a sceptical observer and, at first, the old frontiersman confirmed my expectations precisely — this was to be a lecture by an itinerant showman rather than a scientist. As he began I was put in mind of accounts of American revivalism and circuit riding, indeed some of what Muybridge had to say evoked quacks like R.H. Collyer and his absurd notion of psychography. For Collyer, of course, the photographic apparatus is interconnected with the human nervous system. Where photography can render visible the material but imperceptible vibrations of the ether, the brain can record and capture — in a visual form — thoughts vibrating in this same mediating substance.[10] According to such theories, the brain is then the transmitter and receiver of images, and though the results are altogether questionable, some photographers have determined to capture recordings of thought.[11] Psychical researchers have even speculated that the activity of the brain can induce 'sympathetic vibrations' in other brains — pictures of thought can be transmitted from one and received in the other.[12] In short, there is a burgeoning movement, at least amongst these societies, to understand photography as an entangled media system that integrates the psychic, per-

---

10 Anthony Enns, 'Vibratory Photography', in *Vibratory Modernism,* ed. Anthony Enns and Shelley Trower (Basingstoke: Palgrave Macmillan, 2013), 178.

11 Ibid., 185. See the work of Hippolyte Baraduc.

12 See William F. Barrett, Edmund Gurney and F.W.H. Myers, 'First Report on Thought-Reading', *Proceedings of the Society for Psychical Research* 1 (1882–83): 242. Cited in Enns, 'Vibratory Photography', 180.

ceptual and technical apparatuses.[13] The experiences of this evening compel me to examine this photographic model of consciousness more seriously.

My assumptions concerning Muybridge were first thrown into doubt when it quickly became apparent that the peculiar intensity of his delivery was not a device intended to stir up the audience, but was instead the symptom of a serious malady suffered by our speaker. His voice roiled, as if he was struggling to keep it under control. At times the expressions that gripped his face were disturbingly similar to those worn by the lunatics photographed by Dr Duchenne de Boulogne, and later reproduced in Mr Darwin's book on physiognomy. Why there was no interruption to this contorted performance, I am not sure. I can only say that — like everyone present this evening — I was horrifically rapt.[14]

It is, of course, well known that Muybridge suffered a serious concussion of the front part of the brain so many years ago, but who knows what really occurred after the crash? At his trial there was all that talk of obsessional and irritable behaviour, neurasthenic anxiety and sudden fits of rage. It was said that his hair had turned white over night. I understand that he consulted the noted London physician Dr (now Sir) William Gull on his injuries, and that it was Sir William who prescribed a period of active outdoor convalescence, taken at a distance from the discord and conflict of everyday society.[15] Indeed, the rumour is that it was Sir William who suggested Muybridge take up photography, that he compose himself by composing natural scenes, that he recentre his poise by capturing equilibrial landscapes. Perhaps, instead of through any explicit direction, this curative guidance was applied in the form of sympathetic vibrations — ointment for an injured and malleable brain! After all, it was not so long ago

---

13   Enns, 'Vibratory Photography', 179.

14   Marta Braun, *Eadweard Muybridge* (London: Reaktion Books, 2010), 219; Taylor Stoehr, 'Robert H. Collyer's Technology of the Soul', in *Pseudo-Science and Society in 19th Century America,* ed. Arthur Wrobel (Lexington: The University Press of Kentucky, 1987), 26; Charles Darwin, *The Expressions of the Emotions in Man and Animals* (London: John Murray, 1872).

15   Gordon Hendricks, *Eadweard Muybridge: The Father of the Motion Picture* (London, Secker and Warburg, 1975), 12–13.

that Sir William's name was mixed up in psychic affairs connected with those notorious events in Whitechapel! Naturally, I jest...[16]

In any case, for Muybridge, who was as he reminded us this evening, 'the first photographer the US Army hired directly to document a war', the landscape has its own turmoil, its own conflicts. There are spirits in all lands, he told us — ghost armies, guerilla forces that move invisibly through the ether, like the telegraph messages that transmit reports on war to the rest of the world. The trick to photographing such phenomena, Muybridge told us, is not to be distracted by a search for the spectacle of war but to focus on documenting 'war's raw ingredients', its vibrations, its vectors.[17] It was his intention, he announced, to conduct an experiment this evening to do just that.

Based upon my experience as one of its unwitting subjects, I can say that the experiment seems to have been designed to render the vision of those collected in the auditorium as 'pure' as possible. Employing strange equipment with which I remain unfamiliar, Muybridge isolated the elementary conditions of vision by bathing our retinas in uniform and homogeneous white light. Greatly perturbed by this experience — like most others in the audience — I must admit to enormous difficulty in articulating the results in visual terms. Indeed, I can only echo what my new friend Dr Massumi reported as an 'absence of seeing'. The experiment caused me to enter into something of a fugue, a state of 'unexperiencing' as Massumi so astutely put it, accompanied by a sense of the loss of self... of space... of time. And, of course, it would not be right to suggest that visual perception occurs purified of other senses — with these taken into account... the ordeal intensifies — hallucinations ensue... a fog... a powerful indeterminacy... there is a kind of swimming, not really of objects,

---

16 In 1895, various American newspapers reported that a medium had identified a distinguished London physician as the perpetrator of the 'Jack the Ripper' murders. Speculation has surrounded Gull's involvement ever since.

17 Arthur P. Shimamura, 'Muybridge in Motion: Travels in art, psychology and neurology', *History of Photography* 26.4 (2002): 341–50; Rebecca Solnit, *Motion Studies: Eadweard Muybridge and the Technological Wild West* (London: Bloomsbury, 2003), 104.

but rather, to quote Massumi again, 'a vague, surfacelike field of objectlike or formlike tendency'.[18]

At its foundation, its total field, vision is ... weird. I can only conclude that concrete, objective perception must always launch from this vibratory chaos. It comes later. The actually seen is always, instead, an 'oversight', a reality generated by patterns, rhythms, and movements.[19] Empirical vision transforms the affective intensities swarming 'beneath' the empirical — the endarkenment of the 'infra-empirical' — into habitual vibratory instincts.[20] M. Bergson, who eagerly accosted me as we filed out of the auditorium, described this transformation as perceptual fabulation, where fabulation is a palliative myth, a necessary, though limiting, fiction. Perhaps, then, the photograph as document, as evidence, is precisely a palliative vibration, an anaesthetic fabulation in this sense. It hallucinates the vague shiftings of the total field of vision into actual objects, fusing and establishing truths from chaos, working to anchor and secure an empire of veridical vision. But our perceptual attention is incessantly doubled, backgrounded, by a fugue, by the fog of the imperceptible from which it emerges. Visual experience is, Massumi told us, 'the event of a forced passage from the infra-empirical to the added reality of the empirical, then back ...'[21] Back down into the rabbit-hole of the intensive. My impression is that members of the Society are concerned with another kind of fabulation — an aesthetic ordeal that induces misfires and malfunctions, that falsifies established truths, that cuts the anaesthetic to solicit pain. An ordeal, as Massumi says, in which 'the pain is the beauty (of the world emergent).' Horrific beauty...

LECTURE NOTES of Miss Alice Johnson

Before the commencement of the evening's talk, I was interrogated to a tiresome extent by A.H. — such a tedious woman, must in future avoid — seated to my right. All this was brushed aside, with

---

18 Massumi, *Parables of the Virtual*, 145, 146. This section is inspired by Massumi's essay 'Chaos in the "Total Field" of Vision' from the same volume.

19 Ibid., 155.

20 Ibid., 160.

21 Ibid.

Muybridge's entrance. He certainly cut a fine and imposing figure, wild-haired and bearded in the unruly fashion of a Desert Father or itinerant Messiah, and garbed in broad-brimmed hat and velvet cape as he strutted onto the stage and took up his place at the lectern and by the screen, cutting the air with his pointing stick. I was quite taken aback by his introduction: 'Good evening, I am Muybridge', because I almost thought he would continue with those notorious words, 'I have a message for you…' (!!!) Of course, this immediately brought to mind Frampton's theory that ever since the fateful shooting and murder of a rival in love, almost 23 years ago to the day, Muybridge has been possessed by an ugly spirit which has driven him in the attempt to restore his life's equilibrium, to exorcise this demon to the abyss from whence it came and entered him.[22] This, it is Frampton's intuition, is precisely the explanation for the man's obsession, for his furious generation of untold thousands of image sequences. He was invaded and is unfree from the imperative of stopping time in the bid to echo and overpower the sheer charge contained by the traumatic moment in which the gun was discharged. 'I have a message for you…' Muybridge is the message and the medium, a speeding bullet snatched from time as harbinger of all death, all incursions of the Great Outside.

Indeed, the talk got under way with Muybridge talking those assembled through the minutiae of his working procedure, and the results achieved therefrom, in several such image sequences. Muybridge is an absolutely fascinating speaker, on occasion given to somewhat crude colloquialisms which disrupts and stutters his routines but to overall powerful effect, creating spaces in articulation which mirror and resonate with the spaces between his separate images. At every turn, one is simply never quite certain which direction the discourse will take with the result that every sentence seems to swarm and ring with shadowy unspoken others. At times, Muybridge appeared to be

22 'I submit that that brief and banal action, outside time, was the theme upon which he was forced to devise variations in such multitudes that he finally exhausted, for himself, its significance… So that we might add, in our imagination, just one more sequence to Muybridge's multitude, and call it: Man raising a pistol and firing.' Hollis Frampton, *Circles of Confusion: Film Photography Video Texts 1968–1980* (Visual Studies Workshop Press, 1983), 79.

on the precipice of a great and shattering disclosure to be whispered directly and intimately into the ear. At other times, he seemed as if talking to us from a great distance, quite elsewhere. I also, I must admit, lost track of time. I recall Bergson muttering approvingly of Muybridge's decision to dispense with the animation of his image sequences on this occasion (his true art, said Henri, was the photographic, which admitted the eye into the unseen, the virtual and did not scoop it ever onwards). Then, I was given over to reverie, drifting back in my mind to our recent Eastbourne experiments. Our efforts there were most decidedly influenced by the earlier work of Jan Purkinje, the esteemed Bohemian scientist and Fellow of the Royal Society. Purkinje, of course, professed great admiration of Muybridge's work and its possibilities for advancing morphological and physiological understanding — it is in this very connection that I found myself attracted to this evening's lecture. Purkinje did himself manufacture his own stroboscopic motion picture device, the Phorolyt, and later, its successor, the Kinesiscope and argued persuasively for the merits of these machines in demonstrating the motion of a wide range of phenomena, from the beating heart, to the movement of fluids, from the growth of plants to the progress of battles. Most crucially for our purposes, Purkinje immersed himself in the study of subjective visual phenomena, which he contrived by the exigency of intermittently flashing light — first by candle flame, and later by a variant of his spinning machines — directly into the eyes of his subjects. The effects were remarkable — subjects reported a veritable catalogue of after-image effects and even synaesthetic phenomena. Colour, form, peculiar structures and glyphic formations, all in flux. The potential for such states in facilitating psychical research — specifically, the study of telepathy and extra-sensory perception — was all too clear. And it was under such auspices that I yoked Shelford Bidwell, also Fellow of the Royal Society, into the experiments at Eastbourne. Shelford was already engaged in photic conditioning of subjective states, carried out through his investigations of Bentham's top — a machine for rapidly spinning high intensity flickering light into the eyes, by means of a very bright light bulb placed upon a motorized rotating disc within a box. The subject situates eyes (closed or open) by an aperture into the box and is, in due course, encouraged to detail his or her sensory experience. Bidwell's subjects report 'ghosts', after-images similar to those described by Purkinje. It is my confirmed belief that we have, by these means, accessed a field of vision which is perfused by the ethereal dimension and in which psychical phenomena are to be encountered in abundance.[23] To spin light into the eyes of a subject is to render that subject a medium, in contact with larval becomings, with the action of spirits. It is to render the subject a Seer, capable of picking up and transmitting the correspondences we have delineated so crudely in other, earlier circumstances. How else to explain the spiritual contagion we encountered at Eastbourne? Where, again and again, subjects reported the self-same forms in formation... Where merely to project some thought or image into the flicker was to find it given issue in another's consciousness? And what of the enigmatic background to such visions (and auditions) — the deep blackness that some describe, or, further along, the swirling white fog? It is from such extremes that the paradoxical, oddly formless, forms ensue... reminding one of the distinction between those who inhabit Tsalal, the island of darkness in Poe's Pym narrative, and those who dare to push on into the white vortex... From these reflections, I was pulled back into the lecture hall in a way which chimed in strange fashion with my daydream, by my friend Mudge, seated to Bergson's right. William — poor blind soul — complained of great pains in his head which he attributed to the rhythm of Muybridge's lecture. And, indeed, Muybridge, I now discerned, was working himself into a tremendous lather, urging on his assistant to proceed the slides at an enormous pace. But in place of pictures, there were instead... explosions of sheer light... intermittent illumination of the hall with sun-like force. Muybridge's discourse had degenerated into indeterminate yelps and cries. As he spasmed and fell to the floor in the grip of some grand mal, the evening was brought to its convulsive conclusion. It is all connected, everything. Everything is connected by nothing, by the immense abstraction hovering about all that lives.[24]

---

23 See John Geiger, *Chapel of Extreme Experience.*

24 See Joe Milutis, *Ether: The Nothing That Connects Everything* (Minneapolis: University of Minnesota Press, 2006).

LECTURE NOTES of William Mudge, Esq.[25]

I dictate these notes in the comfort of my rooms. I say comfort, but I will not go so far as to say safety, when nowhere is entirely 'safe' for me now, despite the presence of Hugh, my faithful assistant and scribe. God bless Miss Alice for seeing me home when, considering the state I was in, I could scarcely have managed by myself. I am considerably more grounded now, and will secure myself in my present surroundings with further drafts of brandy should the need arise. Although I attended Muybridge's lecture fully apprised of the risks involved — I went there with the expectation that I might learn something to my advantage precisely in connection with my recent experiences — it is never pleasant and never gets easier to be wrenched so into adjacent realms as if I were a rag doll. Curse this affliction! Bergson's words to me after the lecture were a balm, however, and give me some cause for optimism. I will get onto those shortly, since they demand to be recorded if he will not put them to paper himself, but first I must set down some contextual account of the proceedings earlier in the evening plus associated reflections.

Frampton's musings on Muybridge's career are most worthy of note. Let us start there. He contends that the fellow's work is not, as has often been declared, antagonistic towards time. Obsessed with time, yes, but not ranged against it, or at least against all forms of time. Muybridge excoriates the lower dimensions of temporality; that is, the human. Frampton draws our attention to the early landscapes, pictures from California's Yosemite Valley and suchlike — images, clearly, I have never seen for myself, but which Hugh has described to me and which I gather are suitably magnificent. He says of the waterfalls depicted that they comprise 'images of a strange, ghostly substance that is in fact the tesseract of water: what is to be seen is not water itself, but the virtual volume it occupies during the whole time-interval of the exposure'.[26] Further, in images

---

25 This Mudge is an amalgamation of William R. Mudge, ex-photographer and Second Massachusetts Infantryman, who was shot through the head and lost both eyes at the Battle of Chancellorsville, Virginia, in 1863, and Racine Mudge, who seeks the help of the psychic detective, Dr John Silence, in Algernon Blackwood's story, 'A Victim of Higher Space' (1907).

26 Frampton, *Circles of Confusion*, 76.

made of a Panamanian hunting party, during his Central American sojourn, Muybridge deliberately forces the sighted to inspect human figures that are smudged and smeared beyond their natural boundaries, as if he intended a violent dismantling of the personalities of those depicted. The truth is, in Frampton's view, that the artist sought this blurring of the empirical and the actual in all he did. Muybridge cleaves to what might ordinarily be thought to be impossible in the photographic arts. He intends to seize objects in their entirety. That is, as Bergson would say, and as Frampton intimates, to capture their virtuality, which includes the dimensions of higher space and time. This 'impossible' is also the goal in the San Francisco panorama, and, through an altered approach, in his sequences of animal and human motion.

Muybridge led off his talk this evening with what was, it has to be said, a rather diversionary introduction to a number of motion studies. I found it difficult to engage with his detailed dissection of the various components of the horse's walk, canter, gallop and so forth, interspersed with desultory reference to slides of an art-historical nature. Why will he not directly venture what is at the core of his endeavours?! Why is everything of value these days shrouded in such atmosphere of secrecy?! Spit it out, man! It must be patently obvious to one and all that these studies are not even faintly concerned with people or beasts in themselves or the damnable way in which they move their legs. As they have been described to me, they clearly set out to scrub away faces, identities, places, all the peculiarities of personality and moment. Is not one of the functions of the Cartesian grids precisely to expunge such singularity of character? The goal of the motion studies is to illustrate the inventive, illusionary capacities of the eye. They expose, precisely by disrupting and problematizing it, the eye's complicity in narrative identity, in foisting coherence and continuity upon the chaos and multiplicity of the world![27] The imperative of mundane vision is to sensibly connect together all phenomena, to summon 'time', 'space', 'matter' and 'movement' from the void. Pragmatic human constructs. In fact, let us state it bluntly, the human sensorium is a box of illusions, dedicated to an unconscious

---

27 Frampton, *Circles of Confusion*, 78.

and imaginary falsification of the world about us as 'complete' and intelligible precisely as it appears to be... Muybridge's lesson — why will he not put it to us outright? — is that the eye fabulates; the eye, in partnership with the brain, rushes to paint in every inconvenient gap and chink, to make things fit so that we can confidently venture forth and act in the world. The eye makes reality 'scan', just as the poet compels his fancy to conform to the rules of versification. And this, is it not, is exactly why the Society of Ontofabulatory Research invited Muybridge to speak? What is 'Ontofabulatory Research' and what is its Method? This is exactly their domain (even if Bergson exhibits disquiet and quibbles with the specific inflections they give to this notion, 'fabulatory function', in their usage). Yet still their Secretary, in his opening words, will not aim direct. Muybridge's radical programme — shout it — is the re-institution of the intervals in things, gates outwards, to hobble a dominant vision suborned to unconscious and habitual imperatives which have ceased to serve mankind. His image sequences are scansion's disaster. Not to 'stop' time — no! — but to escape Chronos, the time of the eye's all-too-human scansion. To admit the weirdness of the cosmos, to fold out the mundane senses and force their evolution unto a higher order — this was the inner demonstration concealed by Muybridge's outer demonstration this evening. A demonstration of the mystery and mysticism of a temporality inimical to the human, inimical to the very fabulatory function itself, at least as both Bergson and Muybridge conceive it.

I have already alluded to some of Bergson's leading ideas. This gentleman decries the industrialization of time and space as it manifests itself in a certain cinematographic colonization and canalization of reality. It is true his sympathies lie with Psychical Research rather than Ontofabulatory Research — this was the tenor of his remarks to me after the lecture.[28] For Bergson, we few souls are at war with a scientistic, mathematical metaphysic which believes it best serves

---

28 This account of Bergson's ideas is taken from his Presidential Address to the Society for Psychical Research, London, May 28, 1913, as documented in Henri Bergson, "'Phantasms of the Living" and "Psychical Research"' in *Mind-Energy: Lectures and Essays* (London: Greenwood Press, 1975), 75–103.

mankind's interests but which will not admit of certain facts inconvenient to this belief. In fact, the topic of *interest* is uppermost in Bergson's preoccupations. Science has hitherto, in the manner of the Greeks, pinned all its hopes on the calculability of reality. Everything hinges on measurement. In this belief, it does a great disservice to the mind by reducing it to the brain. Here is the error — the brain, as Bergson has it, is merely an 'organ of pantomime'. The brain, he said, 'directs our thought towards action', its function is reality-alignment and 'in doing this it canalizes, and also it limits, the mental life'. The brain is simply a sensory-motor organ, a collection of mechanisms which concern themselves with movement, gesture and attitude. It is the organ by which our thoughts come into contact and friction with the world of things, by which we attend to and 'insert' ourselves into the world. But the brain is not itself the creator of thoughts and feelings, images and ideas. In fact, it blinkers us as it binds us to the 'direction in which we have to go', a movement and direction which sediments itself through habit into the cerebral cortex. The cerebral mechanism, believing it serves our best interests, masks off, screens out, the greater part of what potentially might be perceived and thought upon. It only calls up to perception what is most relevant to the task at hand and thus it is stupidly utilitarian. If we have sudden moments of 'disinterestedness', as during an accident or similar moment of great intensity, then we are sheared away from mechanical bondage to useful action and can access a more 'panoramic vision'. Perception expands to admit more of the 'immense field of our virtual perceptions' which lies imperceptible on the fringes of our attention. It is at the fringes, of course, where Psychical Research finds its true site of exploration. In short, by what means might the habitual mechanisms of the brain be bypassed in order to access what lies beyond? What disasters of the mechanism can we contrive so that we can be emancipated from slavery to our low, cerebrally engrained 'interests' and can move to fulfill our higher, spiritual interests? And here is where I — and Bergson with me — spy Muybridge's merit in his drive to what I have termed scansion's disaster. From the human to the divine! (But it is not so simple — wait, and I will tell …) Space and time divide us bodily and mentally, but the mind is only partly attached to the body and to this space and time — there is another part which mixes with and encroaches upon others. Here is the possibility of what Bergson calls 'intercommunication' and which we call 'telepathy'. As Bergson has it, 'consciousness overflows the organism'. The organism is, in one way, a disease which roots us in the human. Can we disorganize ourselves? By what accidents? As I shall remind you momentarily, I have personal experience of the kind of accident I posit...

Muybridge knows full well that the photographic frame cuts a slice from reality, and thereby places a limitation upon our perception of reality. However, merely to join up many such slices and run them together in what passes for pictorial 'animation' is not sufficient to overcome this limitation. This, too, he has come to realize. Every cut, every frame, creates a seen and an unseen. But what is unseen is not also utterly absent. The frame does not cease to 'communicate' with what lies outside itself even if might seem to suppress it. What is outside — the Virtual, the Whole, duration — 'insists' in every image, threads through all images and communicates the higher space and time of the spirit to it, immanently. As one commentator has put it, the ethereal spirit — unseen nothingness — which is synonymous with Bergson's duration, 'descends into the system like a spider'.[29] (We begin to suggest the ambivalence we feel towards this circumstance...)

I am talking, of course, of the insights of hyperspace philosophy. It is Hinton, in his articles and romances, who has best articulated the compelling notion of those dimensions beyond the three that together form a kind of prison conditioning human knowledge and the sensory-motor organization of the body. When Frampton speaks of Muybridge's efforts to reach towards the tesseract, he draws on Hinton's neologism for the non-Euclidean geometry of the hypercube. By imagining the tesseract, which is the cube's extension into the fourth dimension (just as the cube is the square's extension into the third) Hinton postulates that we might more readily aspire to the spiritual, ethereal condition of higher spacetime. With our 'flickering consciousness', the contingency of things, their changefulness, is all

---

29 These remarks on the frame lean on Gilles Deleuze, *Cinema 1* (London: Continuum, 2005), 17–19.

that we see of the Mystic Whole, the Aetheric Medium which encompasses and traverses all space and time. Our zoopraxical or cinematographic consciousness is a mere 'flicker-effect...a ticking, a tickling, a tintinnabulation on the edge of our perception of a whole that is ethereal, virtual'.[30] This is the whole — the spider — that with its web, its network, conditions and enables all lower spaces and times.

I can personally testify to the veracity of Bergson and Hinton's philosophical ruminations. And here I come to my own predicament. I was once ignorant of my bondage to lower dimensions, before I took up Miss Alice's invitation to participate in the now infamous 'Eastbourne experiments'. I will not go into the particularities of those experiments — they are well known enough by now. Suffice it to say, that, in the wake of Hinton's invitation to exercise the abstract imagination with the aim of unfolding the tesseract in thought, in addition to the effects of Miss Alice's employment of intermittent illumination to elicit certain psychical states, a condition was created in my body which facilitated temporary passage into the etheric body, that is, the tesseract of my body, as four- or five-dimensioned object. This imagination which surpasses image, this abstraction which exceeds the pictorial capacity of the mind, is the 'scaffold' by which, as Hinton correctly estimated, a person might 'slip' elsewhere, into some adjacency, some fuller state of being. Hinton has insisted, as corrective to his earlier cognitive emphasis on conception, that this is a matter of affect, of feeling — even belief or worship — more than it is of intellection.[31] It is a mystical communion, the soul's part of the mind, that was loosed in me by events at Eastbourne. In this, as I initially rejoiced, my blindness is an irrelevance. There is nothing of this higher spacetime that can be seen, only felt. Only intuited. Once there, one feels oneself to mingle and circulate with beings of other orders, and to communicate. There — I have said it. At Eastbourne I underwent an education which enabled me to travel the dimensions!

Here is the nub...To travel in this manner is to pass over into a realm which promises soul's ease, contact with the Divine. But it

30 Milutis, *Ether*, 51.
31 Srdjan Smajic, *Ghost-Seers, Detectives, and Spiritualists* (Cambridge: Cambridge University Press, 2013), 172–74.

can be horrible, so horrible, too. There rose before me, and plagues me yet, the very great danger of losing myself between dimensions, of surrendering my human frame for wanderings which I fear will soon result in my utter obliteration.[32] Just as I, on such occasions, can think and feel the co-presence of other-dimensional beings, so I am thought and felt in return, by turns to be seduced and repelled. A world of angels which shift into monsters at the drop of a hat![33] Ecstasy and horror combined, salvation and vastation in the One, in the Outside! For this is the fact of the matter... such occasions have not abated since the experiments. They occur with increasing frequency, and my absences from the world we know grow in duration. There are a whole host of subtle triggers which compel my sideways slip. Very often it will be a sound, a rhythm, a particular resonance or vibration. This very evening, as Muybridge's lecture reached its climax, I felt the pressure building in me, first signaled by a terrific migraine. It was the rhythm and cadence of his voice, the rising and falling, and the frequency with which the slides clicked over, experienced by me as fireballs in my mind... Muybridge described a collision, a dreadful accident, and I experienced this accident of space and time, unfolded as tesseract, in my very soul, tugged out of my body and from the lecture hall into that place of temporal and geographical confusion which I have sought to describe. To be stretched over all times and spaces simultaneously, to be transgressed so by hosts of angel-monsters, living-dead blobs... This is my predicament to-

32 'Indescribable shapes both alive and otherwise were mixed in disgusting disarray, and close to every known thing were whole worlds of alien, unknown entities. It likewise seemed that all the known things entered into the composition of other unknown things, and vice versa... Foremost among the living things were inky, jellyfish monstrosities... I saw to my horror that they overlapped, that they were semi-fluid and capable of passing through one another and through what we know as solids. These things were never still, but seemed ever floating about with some malignant purpose. Sometimes they appeared to devour one another, the attacker launching itself at its victim and instantaneously obliterating the latter from sight.' H.P. Lovecraft, 'From Beyond', in *Necronomicon: The Best Weird Tales of H.P. Lovecraft* (London: Gollancz, 2008), 391.

33 Racine Mudge talks of his terror at 'seeing people and objects in their weird entirety, in their true and complete shapes... It introduced me to a world of monsters.' See Algernon Blackwood, 'A Victim of Higher Space', in *Tales of the Mysterious and Macabre* (Feltham: Hamlyn, 1967), 394.

day: I CANNOT CONTROL MY ENTRANCES OR EXITS!![34] Vastation! Muybridge becomes a buzzing, whistling horror. I feel my face and frame distort vortically, whirled into fragments and recombined in the elsewhere. I came to…I had fortunately been undetected in my lapse from mundane reality, since Muybridge himself, I gather, had experienced an episode of his own (akin to mine?) which drew all attention. Bergson saw me shaken and I eventually confessed all, everything I have already imparted to Miss Alice. Bergson proclaimed me blessed — he admonished me to find, with his assistance, some way of controlling my entrances and exits, some way of regularizing the process. And here, perhaps, Muybridge may be my saviour. Some therapeutic, spiritual application of the photographic sequence???? Does he know what he is doing???? In the meantime, there is only alcohol which frustrates the action of the etheric vibrations and keeps me in my body…Enough.

---

34   Ibid., 391.

3 | On paraphotography

Do you begin to see there is no officer there in the darkening room?
— W.S. Burroughs

Est Enim Magnum Chaos
— Arthur Machen

Fabulation and the egregore

Burroughs and Gysin's book of methods, *The Third Mind,* begins in an attic room in the late afternoon, shadows gradually growing at the back of the officer who sits there. The officer, battle-scarred and weary, is instructing 'an audience of any two cadets' — 'Why am I here?' he asks, and immediately answers himself: 'I am here because you are here... and let me quote to you young officers this phrase: "No two minds ever come together without, thereby, creating a third, invisible, intangible force which may be likened to a *third mind*". Who is the third that walks beside you?'[1] The officer is himself an incarnation of the third mind, a tutelary presence watching over and addressing the two cadets but also, oddly and at the same time, springing from their own collusive, in part unconscious, interaction. There are two sources in play here for this idea. The first, explicitly quoted, is Napoleon Hill's best-selling self-help manual, *Think and Grow Rich,* published in 1937, and the second is, unattributed, T.S. Eliot's poem, 'The Wasteland', published in 1922. Burroughs's proclivity for juxtaposing 'sub-standard, mail-order style intellectual sources' such as Hill's book with high literary modernist writers (Eliot and Conrad

---

1   Burroughs and Gysin, *The Third Mind,* 25.

are favourites) is intimately connected with what we have earlier described as a 'low theory' approach.[2] Let us take each source in turn.

Hill's book sets out a sequence of steps which will, if followed assiduously, lead to personal success. Self-improvement is here indissolubly associated with advance in business and the profit imperative. In 1908, perhaps apocryphally, Hill, then a newspaper reporter, was assigned to interview steel magnate, Andrew Carnegie. At that meeting, Carnegie challenged Hill to discover fail-safe formulae for success by means of interviewing five hundred of the wealthiest men in the United States. Hill is cagey about directly identifying the essential secret of power thereby revealed to him (as Burroughs notes, Hill believes readers have to make themselves ready to learn it rather than be handed it undisguised) but it would seem to revolve for the most part around the principle of the 'Master Mind'. The Master Mind is a sort of group mind. So, for example, it is asserted that Henry Ford, one of Hill's interviewees, only amassed his wealth and power 'through his association with Edison, Burbank, Burroughs and Firestone'. Ford and friends may not have conceptualized it in quite these terms, but Hill's lesson is that the Master Mind can be consciously engaged for optimum results, wilfully generated in collaboration with others, a phenomenon that carries and realizes desires fed into it by means of exercises in positive visualization and suchlike. One feathers one's nest in harmonious fellowship with others, in experimentally steering a collective intent. Here, then, Burroughs finds a vital source for the third mind in an eccentric, rather vulgar manifesto for survival of the fittest in industrial nature, overlaid with spiritual pretensions but which leaves individual identity more or less intact. In fact, Hill did himself report spiritual experiences, sensing unseen watchers, Masters ready to dispense occult wisdom. In *Think and Grow Rich,* he speculated that the potential for such wisdom had become democratized in the thirties because the 1929 Crash had levelled the playing field for anyone caring to put his principles and formulae into practice. More recently, Deleuze cast a rather more jaundiced eye upon the spiritualization of business ontology in the contemporary moment when he announced in his 1990

---

2   Phil Baker, *William S. Burroughs* (London: Reaktion Books, 2011), 19.

'Postscript on Control Societies' that the 'most terrifying news in the world' is to hear that 'businesses have souls'.[3]

The line in 'The Wasteland', slightly misquoted by Burroughs, runs, 'Who is the third who walks always beside you?' Eliot's uncanny third, 'gliding wrapt in a brown mantle, hooded', was, he notes, inspired by Sir Ernest Shackleton's account of his doomed 1914–17 imperial trans-antarctic expedition.[4] His ship, *Endurance,* trapped and wrecked in pack ice, Shackleton led a small crew in search of rescue, ultimately traversing South Georgia Island on foot with just two companions. The eerie winter dark is revealed in Frank Hurley's famous flash photography. Eerier still is a matter Shackleton adds ostensibly as an afterthought for the sake of completeness, but which is obviously compulsive, something intangible he must express but for which he deems words scarcely sufficient: 'Providence guided us…I know that during that long and racking march of thirty-six hours over the unnamed mountains and glaciers of South Georgia it seemed to me often that we were four, not three'.[5] Both companions later confirmed experiencing the same feeling, unvoiced at the time. What got them across this frozen wasteland was, they concur, a peripherally perceived spectre, a nameless fourth crew member somehow invoked in a moment of catastrophe. In Eliot's poem, this fourth becomes the third, likely an allusion to the Biblical appearance of the resurrected Jesus, unrecognized, to two disciples on the road to Emmaus.

The third mind — providential, messianic and a boon for business — this is the secret of power, the trick you learn after the crash… Here we might expand our sense of the enigmatic third by recourse to the occult concept of the 'egregore', appropriate given that an indispensable element of Burroughsian low theory is magical lore. The egregore is found in ancient writings in association with the demon. The word 'demon' is now typically associated with evil but at its origins referred to 'any spirit, whether good or evil, that is nei-

3   Gilles Deleuze, *Negotiations* (New York: Columbia University Press, 1995), 181.
4   T.S. Eliot, *Selected Poems* (London: Faber and Faber, 1961), 65.
5   Ernest Shackleton, *South: The Endurance Expedition to Antarctica* (Melbourne: Text Publishing, 1999), 177.

ther divine nor mortal but inhabits the intermediate realm between gods and humans. Thus, even angels belong to the general class of beings known as demons'.[6] The realm of the demon is the realm of mediation. In Plato's *Symposium*, Socrates relates a wise woman's account of the daemonic as mediators of communications between men and the gods: 'Being thus between men and gods the daemon fills up the gap and so acts as a link joining up the whole'.[7] In ancient Jewish belief, both angels and demons, good and bad spirits, were Yahweh's messengers.[8] Jewish ideas (and Christian ideas, including the New Testament) of angels and demons, or 'fallen angels', were hugely influenced by the non-canonical, 'doubtful writings' of the Book of Enoch, several copies of which were, in modern times, found amongst the Dead Sea Scrolls.[9] In one of its oldest parts (circa 300 BC), the book discusses the egregores, or 'Watchers' (derived from the Greek, *egregoroi*, for watchful or wakeful). The Watchers are monstrous rebel angels, descending to earth for miscegenous relations with human women and dissemination of forbidden knowledge, sorcery and technology. From this union emerged hungry and destructive giants or titans.[10] It is in Eliphas Levi's codification of the Western occult tradition, *The Great Secret: Occultism Unveiled* (written in 1868, but published posthumously in 1898) that the concept of the egregore begins to be developed for a more modern context in which they are comprehended in terms of cosmic forces:

> Suns rival suns and the planets exert against planets, in opposing the chains of attraction, an equal energy of repulsion, in order to protect themselves from absorption and to preserve their individual existences. These colossal forces have sometimes taken a shape and have appeared in the guise of giants: these are the egregors of the book of Enoch; terrible beings to whom we resemble the infusoria or microscopic insects which breed between

---

6   Matt Cardin, "A Brief History of the Angel and the Demon", in *Dark Awakenings* (Poplar Bluff, Missouri: Mythos Books, 2010), 187.

7   Cited in ibid., 194.

8   Ibid., 191.

9   Ibid., 192.

10 Ibid., 200.

our teeth and on our epidermis. The egregors crush us without pity because they are unaware of our existence; they are too big to see us and too limited to guess that we are there. This explains the planetary convulsions which engulf whole populations.[11]

Traces of these 'fabled Titans' and their 'barbarous names', are to be found in many magical traditions. Again, they can appear either as black or white, maleficent or beneficent. Nevertheless, most imposing, 'most monstrous' among egregores, is the Devil himself. Writ large in Levi's account is the inhumanness of the egregore, very often manifested in either hostility or indifference.

The concept was taken up by the late nineteenth to early twentieth century occult organization, the Hermetic Order of the Golden Dawn, where it was understood as a virtual form resulting from the ideas and wishes of a group of magical allies. Contemporary chaos magician, Phil Hine, describes the magical egregore as a 'mask of the void', focused upon as a means of both personal and group development. It marks an aspiration to 'become other', opening a 'gateway' through which the adept can move to other states.[12] The egregore's relation to notions of objectivity and subjectivity is uncertain — it occupies the gap between self and other, subject and object.[13] Indeed, such a threshold-entity requires careful ritual husbandry since it rapidly acquires a life of its own.[14] Fellow chaos magician, Pete Carroll, connects the egregore to Rupert Sheldrake's morphic field theory,

---

11 Eliphas Levi, *The Great Secret: Occultism Unveiled* (York Beach, ME: Samuel Weiser, 2000), 127.

12 Phil Hine, "On the Magical Egregore". Available at http://www.philhine.org.uk/writings/ess_egregore.html

13 See Cardin, *Dark Awakenings*, 195, on the ancient uncertainty with regards to the objectivity or subjectivity of the existence of demons.

14 There are numerous instructive examples in fiction. Frank Baker's 1940 novel, *Miss Hargreaves,* for instance, deals, somewhat more prosaically, with the spontaneous creation of an elderly woman during a prank played by two friends which has very undesirable consequences for her controllers. When Miss Hargreaves' troublesomeness reaches a peak, her principal creator exasperatedly releases her to her own devices, whereupon she becomes, in effect, a demon dedicated to destroying his life.

understanding its creation in terms of 'formative causation': 'whenever a new event occurs in the universe, it predisposes all subsequent similar events to occur in the same way by the agency of a "morphic field" ubiquitously across space and time'.[15] Angels and demons are morphic field phenomena initiated by human interaction with cosmic forces, but Carroll explains that animals, in their repetitive behaviours, also spontaneously create egregoric entities. If the human egregore is God, 'magicians consider that all life on this world contributes to, and depends on, a vast composite egregore' which, it is intimated, exceeds God and has been known by many names, including the Devil and Pan.[16]

The third mind, then, can be conceived as an egregore. In fact, egregores are abundantly referred to throughout the corpus of Burroughs's work, if not named as such. Egregores encompass both the friendly officer and the entity described variously as 'Control' or 'The Ugly Spirit', where the latter is, fairly explicitly, of alien derivation. Control is an alien egregore which seeks possession of the human and occupies or exploits the same traumas and catastrophes as Burroughs's officers at the intersection, as Burroughs himself discovered on the occasion of his 'accidental' murder of his wife: 'I live with the constant threat of possession, and a constant need to escape from possession, from Control…the death of Joan brought me in contact with the invader, the Ugly Spirit, and manoeuvred me into a lifelong struggle, in which I have had no choice except to write my way out'.[17]

Burroughs is compelled to write his way out from under the coils of the Control egregore. This is a fabulatory exercise, a fabulation against the possessing fabulation — 'Operation Rewrite', as he occasionally dubs it — which has recourse to Control's skillset and more, a bag of tricks consisting of a range of third mind conducive media forms. As we encounter the weary officer in the darkening attic room, we see on the desk before him his notes, scrapbooks, photographs, tape recorder and typewriter, all of his various ports of

---

15   Peter J. Carroll, *Liber Null & Psychonaut* (York Beach, ME: Samuel Weiser, 1987), 193.

16   Ibid., 194.

17   Burroughs, *Queer*, 18.

entry into intersection. His repertoire consists of media past as well as media present: 'A window shade drawn down serves as a screen for magic-lantern slides'.[18] This calls up a media archaeology, or dark variantology of media, which divulges what horror writer, Thomas Ligotti, calls 'a secret too terrible to know'.[19] We lose ourselves to media, becoming puppets of media rather than users or controllers. The third does not tell a story of the development of positive or lucid media but rather throws out images of fracture in such a master plan, intimating the weirdness, the crawling chaos of lucifugous media life. Media can be conceived as thoroughly egregoric in nature, prone to evolving inhuman lives of their own. Media are themselves threshold-entities, 'gateways' into dimensions of otherness. Operation Documenta, disclosed in our dispatches in Chapter 2 on the intrigue surrounding the work of the Bechers, can be considered an episode in the life of a certain photoegregore, just as Marc Couroux has identified a phonoegregoric entity, a 'shadowy phonic consortium', at the base of contemporary control experiments with earworms and related sonic phenomena.[20] The occult life of egregoric media is a crucial resource for the parasitical schemes of new forms of power. Photography, in particular, is ripe for experimentation with regards to demonic possession: 'There is in fact something obscene and sinister about photography, a desire to imprison, to incorporate, a sexual intensity of pursuit'.[21]

The egregore walks always beside you. It is 'para' in the sense explained by Laura Kurgan. Para, from the Greek for 'beside' or 'beyond', has a shadowy, 'double sense of alongsideness and incompleteness'.[22] Kurgan employs it in relation to empirical method. Where working with data is usually understood as an objective en-

---

18 Burroughs and Gysin, *The Third Mind,* 25.

19 Ligotti, *The Conspiracy Against the Human Race,* 91. The idea of a dark variantology is a riff on Siegfried Zielinski's *Deep Time of the Media: Toward an Archaeology of Hearing and Seeing by Technical Means* (Cambridge, MA: MIT Press, 2006).

20 Marc Couroux, "Preemptive Glossary for a Technosonic Control Society (with lines of flight)', 2014. Available at http://www.xenopraxis.net/MC_technosonic-glossary.pdf.

21 Burroughs, *Queer,* 114.

22 Laura Kurgan, *Close Up At A Distance: Mapping, Technology and Politics* (New York: Zone, 2013), 35.

counter with concrete quantities, the hard facts of reality, she commends instead a para-empirical attitude. Data are never 'raw', never accessed in some pure state. That is, they are always *mediated,* 'always subject … to all the conventions and aesthetics and rhetorics that we have come to expect of our images and narratives'.[23] Data, always mediated, exist beside the world, incomplete. The para-empirical condition is our field of operations. Mediation, the crux of the matter, is para-phenomenal, a site of incompletion and alongsideness. It is the site of a strange resistance and occlusion which harbours the potential for a dark vitality. Just so, paraphotography is the egregore of photography, the daemonic always-beside-you of photography. It is a non-human photography that escapes perfect control.

The 'always-beside-you', egregoric condition is, for us, indissociable from the concept of fabulation. This concept rests with the assumption that reality and fiction, truth and falsehood are intertwined. To falsify the real with metaphors, images or stories is to counter the actual, to evoke virtualities. It is at the heart of the assertive creation and codification of the self and the world over against prior images, prior coding, which in turn compels further movement within the self, self-overcoming, by virtue of a responsiveness to the counter-falsifications of others. Ceaseless alteration of self and world ensues. As Deleuze puts it, the world is falsified and rendered unfinalizable by a 'chain of forgers'.[24] Falsification, or fabulation, to give it Deleuze's preferred name (after Bergson), constitutes a release of life's dissonance, a production of 'truths that "falsify" established truths'.[25] This process is never a matter of identifying contents which are simply true or false but rather of a ramifying world-making, 'false in its form'.[26] Fabulation actualizes a world and lends it consistency whilst validating and refusing to suppress the virtuality of the world. This is not, of course, to say that fabulation is perfectly transparent mediation. It cannot change the world in predictable, controlled

23 Ibid.
24 Gilles Deleuze, *Essays Critical and Clinical,* trans. Daniel W. Smith & Michael. A. Greco (London: Verso, 1998), 101.
25 Daniel W. Smith, "'A Life of Pure Immanence': Deleuze's 'Critique et Clinique' Project', in *Essays Critical and Clinical* (London: Verso, 1998), xxvii.
26 Ibid.

ways. Rather, it trips off the life of alternatives from within the interstices of the actual.[27] In the terms set out here, fabulation is bound up with the creation of egregores.[28]

Fabulation can probably best be explicated by working through the manner in which Deleuze derives and transforms the concept as it appears in Bergson's work.[29] For Bergson, fabulation, or the fabulatory function, is one of the two sources of morality and religion.[30] The insect societies of the anthill or the beehive are stabilized and regulated by natural instinct. They are essentially static and closed. Individual insects have little autonomy. Humans, however, possess intelligence. Intelligence is inventive, creative. It is logical, it identifies causes and effects and it identifies alternatives. Intelligence affords individuals greater autonomy. They can organize themselves much more flexibly and build more open, mutable societies. In fact, and crucially, intelligence poses a *danger* in that, without check, it presents the likelihood of the dissolution of social bonds. In its inventiveness it threatens instability. Society must defend itself against intelligence because, in its apprehension of the fact of impending death, intelligence throws us into despair. In its assessment of cause and effect it is bound to acknowledge that our powers are limited.[31] Fabulation therefore arises as a 'virtual instinct' which serves to socially cement individuals, to foster a sense of moral obligation to those of one's community, to defend that community as a matter of habit and custom: 'Fabulation is an action of the intelligence, yet its basic function is to counteract tendencies that are inherent in intelligence itself.'[32] At root, it manifests a protective hallucination against

27 We have discussed this elsewhere. See Rob Coley and Dean Lockwood, "The Radical Fantastic: Fabulatory Politics in China Miéville's *Cities of 'Lies-that-Truth,'*" *C21 Literature: Journal of 21st-century Writings* 1.1 (2012): 27–44.

28 We acknowledge the Cybernetic Culture Research Unit's work on 'hyperstition', a concept with similar implications to fabulation, and also its use of Burroughs as a conceptual persona. See CCRU, "Lemurian Time War".

29 We are here drawing on Ronald Bogue's account in *Deleuze's Way: Essays in Transverse Ethics and Aesthetics* (Aldershot: Ashgate, 2007).

30 Henri Bergson, *The Two Sources of Morality and Religion* (New York: Doubleday Anchor, 1956).

31 Ibid., 210.

32 Bogue, *Deleuze's Way,* 92, 93.

shocking events, feelings and experiences of disasters. Bergson cites William James's report of his experience of the 1906 earthquake in San Francisco. James felt that the event, far from filling him with terror, fulfilled a warning given him by a friend before his trip to Frisco. So comfortable he even cheers on the destruction, here, then, is the 'quake foretold, shock assuaged in advance, itself like an amusing friend: 'I personified the earthquake as a permanent individual entity', James writes, pointing to a 'living agent as its source and origin'.[33] James also encounters a woman who believes ardently that the 'quake augurs the end of the world and the day of judgement, and secure in this belief is protected from the worst extremity of fear. In both cases, as Bergson comments, 'there comes a defensive reaction in the presence of a sudden and grave peril'.[34] Fabulation, the hallucination of personality and intent, is this defence, feeding into the sensory and into action. It is a palliative refrain, a necessary fiction-as-habit which claims and domesticates the shock, locating 'a mischievous, maybe a malignant being, but still one of ourselves, with something sociable and human about it'. A 'combination of circumstances' is attributed with a 'soul'.[35]

If the fabulatory function — our virtual instinct — is the first source of religion ('static religion'), the second is the *élan vital*, or 'creative emotion'. Fabulation, for Bergson, is fundamentally conservative and tends towards stasis, closing a momentarily ruptured circle. Fabulation protects the human hive. Creative emotion, however, itself constitutes a rupture of fixed structures. It is violent, ushering in the new, the hitherto unknown. This is the source of 'dynamic religion'. Bergson celebrates a 'vital impetus…communicated in its entirety to exceptional men who in their turn would fain impart it to all humanity and by a living contradiction change into creative effort that created thing which is a species, and turn into movement what was, by definition, a stop'.[36] Deleuze's twist on fabulation originates with his insistence on thinking fabulation itself as a matter of 'genuine

---

33 Cited in Bergson, *The Two Sources of Morality and Religion,* 155–56.

34 Ibid., 157.

35 Ibid.,158.

36 Ibid., 235.

creation'.[37] Deleuze does not see fabulation as separate from the perilous event, but rather as entirely at one with it, affirming the opening to the outside, the rupture of the closed circle, which is disaster. Most clearly formulated in *Cinema 2*, in terms of the ethnographic documentary work of Perrault and Rouch, fabulation is the function by which the self invites catastrophe and reinvention. Perrault and Rouch were engaged, in their different ways, in giving 'the false the power which makes it into a memory, a legend, a monster'.[38] Each film-maker, Deleuze writes, 'sets off with the same slender material, camera on the shoulder and synchronized tape-recorder; they must become others, with their characters, at the same time as their characters must become others themselves'.[39] Perrault and Rouch enter into collaborations with subjects from which some third is created, a new community, a mythos, is legended or fabulated. Deleuzian fabulation is, in this account, clearly resonating with the Burroughsian third mind and with the occult concept of the egregore. In this, as Bogue points out, Deleuze is like Bergson in dismissing stories and narration. Fabulation concerns invented personae, egregores, not myths and legends as such. Fabulation rips through the pre-recordings, tears up continuity. What is primary is the image as rip or crash, a particular intersection picture, or, as Bogue puts it, with reference to the cinematic, a sculpting of time-space which stands inside/outside the given.[40] This image achieves magnitude and intensity, becomes a 'giant', and 'lives its own life'.[41] It is most assuredly not a matter of self-projection. It is instead a matter of 'mutual intercession'.[42] The individuality of all collaborators is exceeded in the metamorphic 'becoming-other' of the image. To be party to fabulation is to be a seer, a clairvoyant, opening both oneself and one's reality to its outside, to 'a reverse side consisting of Visions and Auditions'.[43]

37   Bogue, *Deleuze's Way*, 97.

38   Gilles Deleuze, *Cinema 2: The Time-Image* (London: Continuum, 2005), 145.

39   Ibid., 147.

40   Bogue, *Deleuze's Way*, 103.

41   Deleuze, cited in ibid.

42   Ibid., 101.

43   Ibid., 104.

Paraphotography as weird medium

The question of the fabulatory life of the egregore can be pursued, we would suggest, with reference to recent debates within media studies about the life of media. Sarah Kember and Joanna Zylinska have argued that media studies has, overall, organized itself around 'false divisions' — the habit of framing media in terms of dichotomous oppositions. For example, the question of determinacy is presented as a dichotomy. On the one hand, technicists argue for a picture of media as an all-powerful force shaping our lives. On the other hand, there are those who emphasize human agency, the social shaping of media technologies according to social necessities. Kember and Zylinska are concerned to think mediation as a process which is not really captured by these kinds of divisions. There is not the medium on the one hand and society on the other, machine and human in opposition. They are inseparably bound together as part of the same process. It's not that we shape and control media or are shaped and controlled by media. Rather, it is better to begin from the idea that we are ourselves media: 'As we modify and extend "our" technologies and "our" media, we modify and extend ourselves and our environments'.[44] Mediation is onto-genetic, a world-making process, a power through which we become with the world. It is one process, a process which is at the same time, technological, social, economic, biological and psychological. We, the human, are in a process of co-emergence with the non-human, with technology, always already in relation to it, always already, in a sense, outside ourselves. Mediation is therefore a process of creative evolution. We are made and unmade in mediation and it is a mistake to conceive of ourselves as masters, autonomous controllers of this process. As Kember and Zylinska note, 'human creative activity is accompanied by (and often superseded by or even contradicted by) the work of non-human forces'.[45] Through this creative evolution we become what we are. We stabilize our position in the world. Technology means survival, the carving out of territories, the power to act in the world over great distances, to make things happen and make them happen faster. But,

---

44 Kember and Zylinska, *Life After New Media*, 13.

45 Ibid., 22.

ON PARAPHOTOGRAPHY

we are also at the same time destabilized, shaken by change, altered and opened up by the process. Any stability is only transient, a temporary enactment, a temporary fixing — permanence is impossible. As Mark Hansen puts it, 'new media destabilize existing patterns of biological, psychical, and collective life even as they furnish new facilities'.[46] 'What our material history teaches us', Hansen suggests, 'is that human beings evolve in correlation with the evolution of technics; the long line of once-new new media would simply be the index of this coevolution'.[47]

The philosophical perspective Kember and Zylinska use to frame this phenomenon is that of *vitalism* (or, we could say, in Jane Bennett's formulation, *vital materialism*). Vitalism, long out of fashion, has returned with the perceived need to overcome dualistic perspectives, to think media and society, machine and human, material and immaterial, nature and culture *together*. There is not, then, a material reality or material base which has been lost, vaporized by digital media in a process of dematerialization as many technicist approaches suggest. And the 'social shaping of technology' approach, which places greatest importance upon necessities arising from material, social and historical circumstances, equally fails to adequately capture the process of mediation. Vitalism, in its contemporary form, understands both the human and the machine, the cultural and the material, the organic and the non-organic, as vital, as having 'lifeness', inventiveness and agency. Matter is not passive, inert, neutral and neither are media — they are vibrant, lively and forceful. Bennett, along similar lines, advises an ecological approach — don't be tempted to blame and condemn, try rather to engage with the ways in which situations are affected by agency as the effect of complex human and nonhuman forces in assemblage.[48] Kember and Zylinska refer, for their part, to the work of Karen Barad. In Barad's 'agential realism', individuals — subjects and objects — do not precede rela-

46 Mark B.N. Hansen, "New Media', in W.J.T. Mitchell and Mark B.N. Hansen, ed., *Critical Terms for Media Studies* (Chicago: University of Chicago Press, 2010), 173.
47 Ibid., 177.
48 Bennett, *Vibrant Matter*.

tions or 'interactions', rather individuals 'materialize in intra-action'.[49] They never exist apart from their reconfiguration in intra-action. 'Exteriority', Barad argues, emerges 'within relations', through the 'agential cut'.[50]

We know that photography, conceived as arch-representationalist medium, was held in contempt by Bergson and Deleuze. But these thinkers, as Kember and Zylinska insist, are also a resource for challenging representationalism, for thinking photography in terms of the unrepresentable event of mediation rather than in terms of photographic images. We routinely obscure the vitality and dynamism of photography in wedding it so firmly to death and stillness. Photography is one of the ways in which we cut and thereby order and 'tame' the vibratory flux of chaos.[51] For Deleuze, life ceaselessly cuts into itself, becomes other. In other words, it is technological — bringing forth/creating. In foregrounding the cut, photography is close to life. 'All life is photographic'.[52] This is its vitality. Photography intuits time in its cutting. It affords 'fleeting access … to the movement of things'. It allows 'exploration' of life flows 'without drowning'.[53]

Photography, as conceived by Kember and Zylinska, is the production of an ethico-aesthetic incision, which is also an ontogenetic 'process of differentiation and life-making'.[54] As we cut, we 'become-different-from-the-world'. We enact our separateness and we put ourselves into relation with the world. Cutting is vital, is ontological genesis, a form-giving, a selving and a worlding. We cut a form, a self and a world out from the virtual. Only intuition, as opposed to 'ordinary knowledge', allows the process of mediation to be apprehended. Intuition is an immanent, practical 'knowing' rather than

---

49 Adam Kleinman, "'Intra-actions' (Interview with Karen Barad)', *Mousse* 34 (2012): 77.

50 Ibid.

51 See Gilles Delezue and Félix Guattari, *Anti-Oedipus* (London: Continuum, 2004), 38–39: 'Every machine, in the first place, is related to a continual material flow that it cuts into. It functions like a ham-slicing machine, removing portions from the associative flow'.

52 Kember and Zylinska, *Life After New Media*, 84.

53 Ibid., 86.

54 These comments on photography as cutting draw closely on Kember and Zylinska's argument in Chapter 3 of their *Life After New Media*.

a knowledge bound up with the subject-object distinction. It works from within media, inside the life of media rather than handling an inert object. Intuition is a special kind of cutting which is crucial for 'capturing' process. Not ordinary knowing-cutting, nor 'going with the flow', but a different cutting, a 'differential cutting' which does not occlude process.

Citing Barad, Kember and Zylinska suggest that we avoid 'acting on' or 'doing to' the world, and instead seek to 'intra-act', to become with, the world. This is a selving which refuses to step outside phenomena, which always finds itself within, in the middle. The 'agential cut' is a 'temporary stabilization' which, also a connection up with duration and process, is never forgetful of the contingency of its difference and its boundaries.[55] The creative incision is an ethical decision in that it forms self and world in a particular way. The self and the world is born in an act of violence, a surgery or a butchery, but it can be a 'good violence' (Levinas).[56]

Kember and Zylinska have reservations with regards to the concept of media ecologies in contemporary media studies because, as they suggest, approaches foregrounding this have tended to posit relationality as a matter of fact and have not sufficiently engaged with 'minor processes of power', perhaps linked to their affiliation with cybernetics and system theory.[57] They believe they can circumvent this shortcoming in such thinking by mobilizing Barad's notion of the agential cut.[58] Nevertheless, the 'fact' of a prior relational field has seemed strategically important to foreground within recent debates around Speculative Realism and, in particular, Object-Oriented Ontology (OOO). As Michael Goddard claims, these approaches tend to conflate relations with 'correlationism' — the idea that objects exist only insofar as they exist for, and are accessible by, humans. For object-oriented thinkers such as Graham Harman, objects exceed their relations. However, Goddard argues,

---

55 Ibid., 81–83, 187.
56 Ibid., 89.
57 Fuller, cited in ibid., 183.
58 Ibid., 23.

> Harman's proposition of thinking the object in-itself…in a with-
> drawal into its own essence, is…hardly a successful move beyond
> correlationism, since the very term object (as opposed to "thing",
> for example — a thing-oriented ontology would definitely be
> more Lovecraftian!) is meaningless outside of a prior subject/ob-
> ject relational field, and more significantly is contradictory since
> at once posing the object's unknowability, even ineffability, at the
> same time claims that it can be understood outside of its rela-
> tions, and the correlationist relationship in particular.[59]

Effectively extending this critique, Eugene Thacker notes that OOO
(it is its 'central blind spot') 'sidesteps the central problem of objects — that of mediation and its paradoxes, the dual necessity and
opacity of all mediation, not just that of objects in relation to each
other'.[60] This thought promises to take us in a quite different direction to the lines of thinking we identify in Kember and Zylinska's
media vitalism and Goddard's advocacy of media ecologies. Thacker
is close to the kind of thing-oriented ontology that Goddard, tongue-
in-cheek, commends, but what is of particular interest in his work is
neither simply the obscurity of things nor their relationality but rather the *obscurity of relationality* entailed by things. What withdraws is
relationality or mediation itself. Mediation, in Thacker's recent work,
is recessive, strange and dark.

Let's briefly explore this notion of mediation's paradox. On the
one hand, there is something tremendously compulsive and imperative about communication. Life, it seems, is unthinkable without
the promise of communication. On the other hand, however, the
promise of communication always harbours the anxiety of a failure
of communication, or of excommunication. This peculiar 'double
movement' we witness in 'the message that says "there will be no

---

59 Michael Goddard, "Ontogenesis before Ontology: Media Ecologies, Material-
    isms and Objects". Paper presented at the symposium *Secret Life of Objects: Me-
    dia Ecologies*, Rio de Janeiro, 5 August 2015. Available at http://www.academia.
    edu/14766299/Ontogenesis_before_Ontology_Media_Ecologies_Material-
    isms_and_Objects.

60 Thacker, "Dark Media', 115.

more messages"' is central to Thacker's thinking about mediation.[61] The effect is an endarkenment of all mediation. All media become 'dark media', thrust from comforting assumptions about a 'vitalistic, communicational flux and flow' into a much stranger place in which there is something hidden and confounding, some blindness, or 'shadowy absence at the core of all mediation', which plunges us into doubt.[62] Thought of this way — and this is the closest we will get to a clear definition of dark media — media's true function is to 'make accessible the inaccessible — in its inaccessibility'.[63]

In this, we are not really dealing with a failure of communication as such. In fact, when we contemplate dark media, Thacker is at pains to point out, mediation 'strangely seems to work all too well'.[64] It fulfils its role consummately. This is particularly evident in supernatural horror fiction, the success of which hinges precisely upon articulating convincing instances of access to the inaccessible. Take, by way of an example, Arthur Machen's tale, 'The Great God Pan', one of the foundation stones of the genre of weird fiction, which concentrates upon a revelation of the 'abyss of all being'.[65] The tale concerns the results of an experiment in occult science by one Dr Raymond. By a combination of alchemy and brain surgery, Raymond succeeds in breaking open 'the door of the house of life' and exposing a young woman to the jeopardy of an encounter with whatever 'might pass forth or enter in'.[66] This is conceived, in the tale, as a visit with the god Pan, an experience both of panic terror and ecstasy. It is a communication which bridges 'the unutterable, the unthinkable gulf that yawns profound between two worlds'.[67] 'ET DIABOLUS INCARNATUS EST. ET HOMO FACTUS EST', an inscription tells us: the experiment is wildly successful and from the encounter, a child is born into the world who

61 Ibid., 80.
62 Ibid., 81, 84.
63 Ibid., 96.
64 Ibid., 92.
65 Arthur Machen, "The Great God Pan', in *Late Victorian Gothic Tales,* ed. Roger Luckhurst (Oxford: Oxford University Press, 2005), 228.
66 Machen, "The Great God Pan', 232.
67 Ibid., 185.

incarnates Pan in human form.[68] This human bridge which spans the abyss, who grows to become 'at once the most beautiful woman and the most repulsive', is Helen Vaughan, contact with whom will bring ruin and death to all men who succumb to her spell.[69] She is a paradoxical being, 'the terror that may dwell in the secret place of life, manifested under human flesh; that which is without form taking to itself a form'.[70] When she is eventually confronted and vanquished, she undergoes transformation from woman to man to animal to jelly, all as the room darkens, but not with 'the darkness of night', rather, as a witness reports, with a 'negation of light; objects were presented to my eyes, if I may say so, without any medium'.[71]

Here we have mediation as a 'bare activity', 'a mediation that almost immediately negates itself'.[72] For Thacker, drawing the distinction between objects and things, the horror of mediation, abundantly expressed in the fiction of horror, is that objects of mediation undermine the whole deal in their withdrawal, in their thingly inaccessibility. Unlike objects, things are not for humans, not possible, positive or available. It is precisely in their unavailability that things come alive. This is a kind of vitalism, but not a vitalism of fullness, of proliferation in the sense of the immanence of multiplicity. It is a *dark* vitalism, a vitalism of the negative, the void, the immanence of indistinction.[73] Objects come alive when they pass into the darkness of things. Media objects recede, 'often to the point that the object becomes itself vitalistically lifelike and animate. There is, perhaps, a strange life of media that is equivalent to the slippage from "objects" to "things"'.[74] This coming to life occurs with the annihilation of the

---

68 Ibid., 196.

69 Ibid., 202.

70 Ibid., 225.

71 Ibid., 228–29.

72 Thacker, "Dark Media", 105.

73 Ibid., 127. Thacker portrays this negative immanence of indistinction with reference to Laruelle's notion of the One. For an extended account of this, see Alexander Galloway's *Laruelle Against the Digital* (Minneapolis: University of Minnesota Press, 2015). We would add that negative immanence might also be fruitfully explored with reference to Austin Osman Spare's principle of the 'Neither-Neither' — see Spare's *The Book of Pleasure* (1913).

74 Thacker, "Dark Media", 139–40.

middle, the negation of mediation.[75] If we can still talk of ecologies, we are here dealing with a peculiar, weird ecology, not an orgy of promiscuous connectivity, but an abyssal, shadowed ecology, silent and still. Ontogenetic abyss rather than cut and flow. With dark media, we are entangled with the weird relation of annihilated relation. The advent of the weird is when what looms is the abyss between realms, between two different ontological orders, an 'impasse' in which things are apparently absent or invisibly present and in which subject and object, sender and receiver, are dissolved.[76] The weird names a paradoxical relation in which there is only the abyss, only the middle, but if there is only this then it is itself negated as middle. What of the human? We are entangled with things living, feeling, thinking and acting in ways we cannot comprehend, with demonic vitality, possessed and possessing. An ecstasy of possession in which we become indistinct from things, frozen and silent in thingly fashion.[77] Possessed by the unhuman, our feelings, actions and thoughts become strange to us.

In our dispatches, we have conceived a paraphotographic practice as situated within — embedded within — a war universe, as consisting of a bag of tricks for fighting 'Control'. A low theory, a practice of ontofabulatory images or fragments, which, as it portrays, casts a spell, enacting egregores against the Control egregore. Mediation is egregoric, bringing subjects and objects to a passage by which they become unhuman things, strange life. On the one hand, Control's egregore centres on the captivation of life as teeming riot, promiscuous edit-flow, the vectoral production of new worlds of value. On the other hand, there is mooted the paraphotoegregore — the connection which cuts to reveal not new worlds but the abyss (lost in the cut as in space). Burroughs was particularly fond of evoking panic terror at the moments at which the pre-recorded universe, the 'Garden of Delights' or 'GOD universe', is rent apart in a mediatic apocalypse: 'Zigzagging he opened up with camera gun and static — Towers and ovens went up in a nitrous blast of burning film — A great rent tore

---

75   Ibid., 136.
76   Ibid., 133.
77   Ibid., 136.

the whole structure of the garden to the blue sky beyond — He put the flute to his lips and blue notes of Pan trickled down from the remote mountain village of his childhood'.[78] We read Burroughs's career in cut-ups as an extended experiment with weird ecology, an intersection mythos in which intersections are mapped and portrayed in order to reveal the intersection as abyss, to lose ourselves in the darkness and silence of the intersection as indistinction, impossible crossroads. The horror of the crossroads at which all roads recede, disappear into fog or shadow. Ontofabulatory dispatches connect to and cut into flow in order to expose the vegetal riot of Control and to bring it to standstill, ontogenetic abyss.

We suppose that something is missing in photography, despite the clarity of the contemporary image. Paraphotography extends an invitation to a space in-between, a middle after the media. Desire has drained from media. Photographic refrains now operate as part of the 'practical constraints' of an anti-revolutionary, anhedonic system, its social practices fully and invisibly integrated within an informational system which maintains the stable reiteration of capitalistic subjectivity.[79] This is not to say that the reality produced by such refrains is fixed, but rather that carefully mediated photographic networks act as capital's probe-heads, capturing speculative images of future realities by integrating them within an unchanging present, a present reduced to 'infernal alternatives'.[80] This mode of photography anaesthetizes against the painful thresholds of social excesses, it is, as Siegfried Zielinski suggests, 'at the greatest possible remove from what whips us into a state of excitement, induces aesthetic exultation, or triggers irritated thoughts'.[81] In this space of nihilism, of vectoral control, of the enclosure and foreclosure of the virtual, belief in the world lies in tatters. 'Off the hinges' of the world, it is impossible to change the world directly, to step into another world. When the virtual becomes the 'primary mechanism of oppression', we reach instead, with Alexander Galloway, for Deleuze's 'concept

---

78 Burroughs, *The Ticket That Exploded*, 20.

79 Zielinski, *Deep Time of the Media*, 19.

80 Philippe Pignarre and Isabelle Stengers, *Capitalist Sorcery: Breaking the Spell*, trans. Andrew Goffey (Basingstoke: Palgrave Macmillan, 2011).

81 Zielinski, *Deep Time of the Media*, 19.

of the whatever'.[82] We 'demilitarize'. We 'stand down'.[83] The spaces which exemplify nihilism are spaces of possibility for reflexively apprehending our link to the world and repairing belief but the way to this is not, as we may think, through decisive action.

Where photography courts philosophy, paraphotography thinks practically. It is to photography what 'low theory', as identified by Wark, is to philosophy proper. It is low because it is superfluous, uncalled-for; it concerns the reality of the unseen, that which exceeds or withdraws from photography. For Wark, philosophy is paralyzed by the disappointments of failed revolution. A traumatized victim of a bloody accident, philosophy does little more than puzzle over its dismemberment. As a product of grey media, the radical potential of photographic powers is rendered similarly feeble, no longer capable of producing upheaval. *Low* theory, Wark says, is 'negative', a political tactic for exposing false promises, false beliefs, revealing 'the void between what can be done and what is to be done.'[84] But this is still too positive, too affirmationist, recoding the negative on the basis of the subject's inventive potential, on the production of the new. Paraphotographic belief concerns a different void, that is, something of this third nature which remains beyond mediation. When you are being tricked, there is something that does not reveal itself in total, there is always a blind spot, 'a shadowy absence at the core of all mediation', and thus, space for potential.[85]

Paraphotography transfigures the human point of view into what Thacker calls 'the unhuman orientation of deep space and deep time.'[86] Here belief functions beyond the onto-theological culture of the human and becomes an onto-fabulatory exercise, one that is neither moral nor metaphysical but *cosmic*. Paraphotographic practice is akin to demonic possession, to a limit experience Thacker associates with 'dark media'. As he describes it, the 21st century is characterized by the continual confrontation with 'an absolute limit to our ability to adequately understand the world', a phenomenon that is also

82 Alexander R. Galloway, *The Interface Effect* (Cambridge: Polity, 2012), 138.

83 Ibid., 143.

84 Wark, *The Beach Beneath the Street*, 156.

85 Thacker, "Dark Media', 84.

86 Thacker, *Cosmic Pessimism*, 13.

fundamental to the horror genre.[87] Alongside our subjective, human-centric world, we acknowledge an objective nonhuman world-in-itself that exists in an 'already-given state', that is, until the very moment that we perceive it, that we train our lens upon it, and transform it into a world for us.[88] Horror confronts a third category beyond the subjective and objective world — a world without the human. This is a horror of *negation,* paradoxically revealing to us a world 'after' the human. Critical horror, like this, exceeds human emotion to deal in confrontation with the very limits of the human. It is in this sense that paraphotography can be called a dark media stratagem, a mode appropriate to a media culture that is no longer understood on the basis of human senders and receivers, and no longer aimed toward rendering the inaccessible accessible. Rather, it is a practice imma-nent to the paradoxes of mediation, aiming to reveal 'inaccessibility in and of itself', or in Thacker's terms, to 'make accessible the inacces-sible — in its inaccessibility.'[89] Instead of affirming a productive im-manence, an 'always-more-in-the-world' that remains preemptively captured by contemporary power, paraphotography's aesthetic inef-ficacy, or *weird* efficacy, concerns a negative immanence — an im-manence that, as Thacker says, remains 'all pervasive' — immanent with and to itself — just as it remains 'absolutely inaccessible.'[90] The truth of paraphotography is based on successive negations — on fail-ures — on the expression of a limit that can only be articulated as something beyond, something unutterable, unnameable. Here, the risk is that, in communicating the gulf, the void, this 'nothingness' leaves us stranded in the middle, entirely ungrounded. We might though remember that Deleuze stresses the importance of such impossibilities to the creation of possibilities — bottlenecks and cramped spaces are the conditions in which fabulations must oc-cur. Cosmically cramped, paraphotographic belief is, then, an occult practice, a critical horror which is a question of style, of adopting an ethico-aesthetic sensibility to relations with a cosmic outside.

---

87 Thacker, *In the Dust of this Planet,* 1.

88 Ibid., 5.

89 Thacker, "Dark Media", 96.

90 Ibid., 127.

For those in the field

- First things first — it's easy to forget there's a war on. Here words are trapped, webbed up, because pre-scripted even as they occur to you. This is a photography trap because already photographed before the click. A monstrous communicational network (vines, tentacles, coils) to which we are immanent, embedded. The 'front line', deep inside (everywhere)/encrypted (in plain sight).

- Within media ecologies, subjects and objects flow, stabilize and are cut out to flow again, to proliferate and connect. So it goes. But remember that these are only the shallows, so to speak; this is only the dayside. Your job is to discover things nightside, discover your redundancy in a flash photography which suspends all operations in a general blindness. In the field, as officers and cadets of the Paraphotography Corps you have accepted the assignment at the end of which all assignment is defeated.

- Units must be on the look-out for the point of insertion, the crash at the intersection (not always conspicuous). When you find it, step out and take the hit/shot. Congratulations — sightless, you'll catch a glimpse of the swell that has carried you along (all along). No time to surf, units, there's work to do.

- Your useless but fantastic weapon — photography weapon, whatever weapon (it's not yours) — already intimates (has always intimated) the trench beneath the swell. Void the intersection and, pure middle, it voids and possesses you. Descend into this still and silent abyssal indistinction. Lurk far below the connective flow. Entrenched, your unit is rubbed out. Feel free to panic (who's panicking?).

- Await extraction. *You* can't come back, but something (Nada) can. Cresting the wave, you are alien, an intrusion. You are egregore. Everything you touch will fail, crash, reel in horror. No service medal. No glory.

Coda

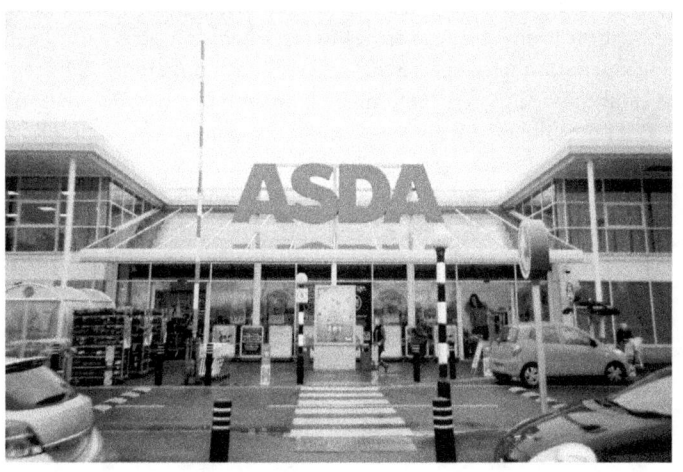

Negative exposure. Last autumn, against our better judgement, and at great personal cost, we successfully reestablished contact with Nova agent Brenda Dunks. Having long departed her offices on Fulham Road (it would seem even Nova agents are subject to the forces of gentrification), Brenda's new cover apparently involves running a photo centre at a branch of the supermarket chain Asda. Following advice, we visited the photo centre on a Friday afternoon, during which time we saw no sign of Brenda's sidekick, Willy Deiches, and thought it prudent not to ask as to his whereabouts. We had been informed, through a source that will remain anonymous, that Brenda still claimed to be in communication with Control, and that she would be willing to facilitate a kind of dialogue (for an appropriate fee, naturally). However, unlike the documented experiences of William Burroughs, Brion Gysin, and Anthony Balch, where questions to Control were typed out and fed into a computer, here, we were told, our questions should take the form of photographs — latent images that beg a developed response. Brenda seemed to recognize us immediately. Clumped into a once white lab coat, its press-stud buttons fastened awkwardly high, her eyes locked on to us as we approached the scruffy counter she commanded. We offered up 27 exposures, housed in a plastic disposable camera, which she accepted with fingers raw and reticulated, perhaps from repeated contact with an unpleasant mix of darkroom chemicals. We were told to return in an hour, a period of time we spent pacing nervously in the carpark.

Light leaks. We made our way back to the photo centre the moment the allotted time had run down. As we arrived, a digital minilab was noisily throwing small piles of glossy prints into a sorter mechanism, but Brenda had already flipped up the counter hatch, pulled aside a black curtain, and was ushering us past the machine towards a darkroom at the rear. A whiff of stale chemistry hung in the air. The cramped space was lit by red safelight and our eyes adjusted slowly to a room piled with photographic apparatus most likely imported from some other space. Piles of grubby print trays lined the workbench. A series of glass and plastic bottles with encrusted lids filled the shelves. A collection of measuring cylinders stuffed into a wash tank with perished hosing occupied much of the floor. A rusty film drying cabinet, wedged into the corner and repurposed as storage, was stacked with paper boxes bearing familiar brand names. Water was flowing freely into a filthy sink. Brenda pulled on a cord that exposed the room to white light, revealing its grime in harsh detail, and drawing our attention to the walls for the first time. Here, rendered in differing sizes and often overlapping each other, were a multiplicity of crude line drawings seemingly depicting people holding cameras. Some were drawn in marker pen, some wiped onto the wall with a thick grease, some scratched into the plaster itself and daubed in a rust-like colour. For a moment we gazed at this parietal graffiti until Brenda broke our reverie with a grunt followed by a gesture to the baseboard of an old enlarger, upon which sat an unsoiled photo wallet bearing the Asda logo. The wallet was stuffed with prints.

Sacred horror. Perhaps precipitately, I immediately open the wallet and fan several of the prints over the baseboard. Beneath the sound of the water gargling in the sink, I am distracted by a strange grunting noise. It sets the cabinet rattling and dust puffs up into the light. No-one else appears to notice. As I take a glimpse at the uppermost print, the noise turns into a low rumble. I see figures I recognize. In the deepest pit of the caves at Lascaux, the perilous chasm once described by Georges Bataille as the 'holiest of holies', there is a twenty thousand year old image of a man beside a bison, both apparently dead or dying. The bison, rendered with remarkable naturalism, has been eviscerated with a spear, its bowels dangling in coils. The man, just a childish cartoon, lies with erect phallus, arms outstretched. His head thrown back, the face is concealed by a bird mask. Here on the print are those same figures, now partially obscured by a swimming film of odd coloration. The noise builds to a roar, my innards boil in sympathy. Darkness radiates from the print, now perfectly black. 'Do this somewhere else, pal'. Brenda sweeps the prints together and jams them into the wallet, pushing us back towards the curtain and out of the darkroom in almost the same movement.

What was the question again? Still tacky, some of the prints resist easy separation. It's as if they wish to overcome their discontinuity. What a peculiar mantic game. 'What was the question again?' I ask.

Base materialism. Rob mutters something about new weapons, pragmatic techniques of resistance. But this print I hold in my hand now, there's a shadowy form in there that brings Gysin to mind. And Gysin is speaking... 'a good deal of these texts become absolutely *unreadable, nobody* could read them, you just — *William himself* said he couldn't read them a second time...uh, they produced a certain kind of very unhappy psychic effects...there was no question of their *efficacity,* but, uh, for what one would use such a thing, uh, gave pause for thought...'[1]

In the middle. There are at least two types of middle, two modes of encounter with an immanent beyond. There is a middle of pragmatics and a middle of horror. The middle of pragmatics is a noisy middle, a busy, multiplicitious realm, an encounter with which produces new connections with the world. It is a space from within which we can map out new possibilities, new transformations to everyday experience. The middle of horror is quite different. It is a space of silence, it is abyssal. It is, as Bataille put it, 'a gaping void'. Nothing pragmatic is gained in an encounter with this middle. The only connection produced is one with a primordial disconnection. The only possibility on offer is impossibility. To encounter this middle is to render ourselves nothing, to sacrifice what is human in us, to sacrifice 'us'.

Drawing with shit. There was no utility to these photographs, they offered no answers, they revealed nothing — even by accident — that might conceivably be turned to our advantage. We could, then, take no hope from these photographs, no promise of escape, we could see no programme of action concealed within them. They were instead grotesquely useless — obscenely, sickeningly unambiguous in their excess. They were photographs that seemed to take the elevated source of the medium — *light* — and reveal something impossibly rotten, a putrid origin. Clutching the wallet of prints, we emerged from the darkroom to find an implausibly large number of customers

---

1   Gysin, *Here to Go,* 51.

gathered at the photo centre counter. Ignoring the queue barriers, this crowd swayed and jostled for Brenda's attention, brandishing their memory cards, beckoning her with USB sticks. Their collective murmur channeled the buzz from a small glass fronted fridge, packed with long out of date film, set beside the cash register. We pitched chaotically into bodies.

Holiest of holies. Out at the back of the store, Brenda makes her way to the bins. Shuffling arthritically through a litter of cheese and cakes rejected by discriminating freegans, she hoists a large box of uncollected snaps to her shoulder in readiness to tip it into the nearest bin. A slight movement amongst the rubbish at her feet snags her attention. She bends to look, distractedly spilling some of the contents of the box which merely add to a substantial heap of prints, all perfectly black, already amassed on the ground. Surprisingly, from amidst these protrudes a phallus, engorged and shining. Never one to pussyfoot, Brenda pushes through the heap and uncovers the naked body of a man, dead or dying. Filthy and emaciated, the man wears a bird mask.

USELESS USELESS   THE END

Smell of developer fixer bison breath

joy joy joy joy you better run the best shots

black slime into the ditch into the pit into the darkroom officers poets.

A loud false click. Human laughter. Animal hit.

ENTER DEATH CLICK NOTHING TO BE DONE CLICK

Coagula negative seeing flatter than the sky

aaaaaghahahahaaghmuahhhhghuhu

SHICK KA-CHICK SHICK KA-CHICK SHICK KA-CHICK HEHEHE

FACELESS FACELESS horse shitter direction in which we go THE EXIT

white fog planetary convulsions

MAGNUM CHAOS BRACE BRACE

SACRIFICE

Brenda grasps the black beak, tugs off the mask. Through the matted hair curtaining his face she recognizes Willy, even though the ecstasy of communication has made him younger.

Bibliography

Allmer, Patricia, and John Sears. *Taking Shots: The Photography of William S. Burroughs.* Munich, London and New York: Prestel Verlag, 2014.

Baker, Phil. *William S. Burroughs.* London: Reaktion Books, 2011.

Ballard, J.G. "'Not entirely a journey without maps': J.G. Ballard on The Atrocity Exhibition'. In *Extreme Metaphors: Interviews with J.G. Ballard 1967–2008,* edited by Simon Sellars and Dan O'Hara, 477–62. London: Fourth Estate, 2012.

———. *War Fever.* London: HarperCollins, 1990.

Barber, Stephen. *Muybridge: The Eye in Motion.* Chicago: Solar Books, 2012.

Barrett, William F., Edmund Gurney and F.W.H. Myers. 'First Report on Thought-Reading'. *Proceedings of the Society for Psychical Research* 1 (1882–83): 13–34.

Barron, Laird. *The Beautiful Thing That Awaits Us All and Other Stories.* San Francisco: Night Shade Books, 2013.

Baxter, Jeannette. *J.G. Ballard's Surrealist Imagination: Spectacular Authorship.* Surrey: Ashgate, 2009.

Benjamin, Walter. *Selected Writings, vol. 4, 1938–1940,* edited by Howard Eiland and Michael W. Jennings. Cambridge, MA: Harvard University Press, 2003.

Bennett Phillips, Stephen. *Margaret Bourke-White: The Photography of Design 1927–1936.* The Phillips Collection, 2003.

Bennett, Jane. *Vibrant Matter: A Political Ecology of Things.* Durham: Duke University Press, 2010.

Bergson, Henri. *Mind-Energy: Lectures and Essays.* London: Greenwood Press, 1975.

———. *The Two Sources of Morality and Religion.* New York: Doubleday Anchor, 1956.

Blackwood, Algernon: *Tales of the Mysterious and Macabre*. Feltham: Hamlyn, 1967.

Bogue, Ronald. *Deleuze's Way: Essays in Transverse Ethics and Aesthetics*. Aldershot: Ashgate, 2007.

Braun, Marta. *Eadweard Muybridge*. London: Reaktion Books, 2010.

Breton, André. *Manifestoes of Surrealism*. Ann Arbor: University of Michigan Press, 1972.

Brookman, Philip. *Eadweard Muybridge*. London: Tate Publishing, 2010.

Burke, Carolyn. *Lee Miller: A Life*. Chicago: University of Chicago Press, 2007.

Burroughs William S., and Malcolm McNeill. 'The Unspeakable Mr Hart'. *Cyclops* 1–4 (July–October 1970).

———. *Ah Pook is Here, and Other Texts*. London: Calder & Boyars, 1979.

———. *Burroughs Live: The Collected Interviews of William S. Burroughs 1960–1997*. Edited by Sylvère Lotringer. New York: Semiotext(e), 2001.

———. *Letters 1945–59*. London: Penguin Classics, 2009.

———. *Nova Express: The Restored Text*. Edited by Oliver Harris. New York: Grove Press, 2014.

———. *Queer*. London: Picador, 1986.

———. *Rub Out the Words: Letters, 1959–1974*. Edited by Bill Morgan. London: Penguin, 2012.

———. *The Ticket That Exploded: The Restored Text*. Edited by Oliver Harris. London: Fourth Estate, 2010.

——— and Brion Gysin. *The Third Mind*. London: John Calder, 1979.

Caillois, Roger. *The Edge of Surrealism*. Durham and London: Duke University Press, 2003.

Cardin, Matt. *Dark Awakenings*. Poplar Bluff, MO: Mythos Books, 2010.

Carroll, Peter J. *Liber Null & Psychonaut*. York Beach, Maine: Samuel Weiser, 1987.

Castaneda, Carlos. *Journey to Ixtlan: The Lessons of Don Juan*. Harmondsworth: Penguin, 1974.

Catling, B. *The Vorrh*. Croydon: Honest Publishing, 2007.

Clegg, Brian. *The Man Who Stopped Time: The Illuminating Story of Eadweard Muybridge – Pioneer Photographer, Father of the Motion Picture, Murderer.* Joseph Henry Press, 2007.

Coley, Rob, and Dean Lockwood. 'The Radical Fantastic: Fabulatory Politics in China Miéville's *Cities of "Lies-that-Truth."' C21 Literature: Journal of 21st-century Writings* 1.1 (2012): 27–44.

Collings, Matthew. *This is Modern Art.* London: Weidenfeld and Nicolson, 1999.

Conekin, Becky E. 'Lee Miller's Simultaneity: Photographer and Model in the Pages of Inter-war Vogue'. In *Fashion as Photograph: Viewing and Reviewing Images of Fashion,* edited by Eugenie Shinkle, 70–85. London: I.B. Tauris, 2008.

———. *Lee Miller in Fashion.* London: Thames and Hudson, 2013.

Conradie, C Jac. et al. *Signergy.* Amsterdam and Philadelphia: John Benjamins Publishing, 2010.

Couroux, Marc. 'Preemptive Glossary for a Technosonic Control Society (with lines of flight)'. 2014. http://www.xenopraxis.net/MC_technosonicglossary.pdf.

Cybernetic Culture Research Unit (CCRU). 'Lemurian Time War'. In *Retaking the Universe: William S. Burroughs in the Age of Globalization,* edited by Davis Schneiderman and Philip Walsh, 274–91. London: Pluto, 2004.

Darwin, Charles. *The Expressions of the Emotions in Man and Animals.* London: John Murray, 1872.

Deleuze, Gilles. *Cinema 1: The Movement Image.* London: Continuum, 2005.

———. *Cinema 2: The Time-Image.* London: Continuum, 2005.

———. *Essays Critical and Clinical.* Translated by Daniel W. Smith & Michael. A. Greco. London: Verso, 1998.

———. *Francis Bacon: The Logic of Sensation.* London and New York: Continuum, 2004.

———. *Negotiations.* New York: Columbia University Press, 1995.

——— and Félix Guattari. *Anti-Oedipus.* London: Continuum, 2004.

———. *A Thousand Plateaus.* London: Continuum, 2004.

———. *What is Philosophy?* New York: Columbia University Press, 1994.

———— and Claire Parnet. *Dialogues II*. London: Continuum, 2006.

Dillon, Brian. *Ruin Lust: Artists' Fascination with Ruins, from Turner to the Present Day*. London: Tate Publishing, 2014.

Eliot, T.S. *Selected Poems*. London: Faber and Faber, 1961.

Enns, Anthony, and Shelley Trower, eds. *Vibratory Modernism*. Basingstoke: Palgrave Macmillan, 2013.

Fisk, Robert. 'Please, Sam, we'll pay you not to play it again'. *The Independent*, 2 June 1993.

Forbes, Peter. *Dazzled and Deceived: Mimicry and Camouflage*. New Haven and London: Yale University Press, 2009.

Frampton, Hollis. *Circles of Confusion: Film Photography Video Texts 1968–1980*. Rochester, NY: Visual Studies Workshop Press, 1983.

Fuller, Matthew, and Andrew Goffey. *Evil Media*. Cambridge, MA: MIT Press, 2012.

Galloway, Alexander R. *The Interface Effect*. Cambridge: Polity, 2012.

————, Eugene Thacker and McKenzie Wark. 'Execrable Media'. In *Excommunication: Three Inquiries in Media and Mediation*. Chicago and London: University of Chicago Press, 2014.

Garlick, Hattie, and Johnny Howorth, dirs. *Don's Last War*. The Times, 2012. https://vimeo.com/56683563.

Geiger, John. *Chapel of Extreme Experience: A Short History of Stroboscopic Light and the Dream Machine*. Brooklyn: Soft Skull Press, 2003.

————. *Nothing Is True Everything Is Permitted: The Life of Brion Gysin*. New York: The Disinformation Company, 2005.

Goddard, Michael. 'Ontogenesis before Ontology: Media Ecologies, Materialisms and Objects'. Paper presented at the symposium *Secret Life of Objects: Media Ecologies*, Rio de Janeiro, 5 August 2015. http://www.academia.edu/14766299/Ontogenesis_before_Ontology_Media_Ecologies_Materialisms_and_Objects.

Goya, Francisco. *The Disasters of War*. Edited by Philip Hofer. New York: Dover, 1967.

Gysin, Brion. *Here to Go: Planet R-101*. Edited by Terry Wilson. London: Quartet Books, 1985.

Hansen, M.B.N. *Feed-Forward: On the Future of Twenty-First Century Media*. Chicago: University of Chicago Press, 2015.

Harris, Oliver. 'The Future Leaks Out'. In *Nova Express: The Restored Text by William S. Burroughs*. New York: Grove Press, 2014.

Heap, Jane. *Machine-Age Exposition Catalogue*. New York: The Little Review, 1927.

Hendricks, Gordon. *Eadweard Muybridge: The Father of the Motion Picture*. London, Secker and Warburg, 1975.

Herr, Michael. *Dispatches*. London: Picador, 2002.

Hine, Phil. 'On the Magical Egregore'. (n.d.). http://www.philhine. org.uk/writings/ess_egregore.html.

Hunt, John Dixon. *Greater Perfections: On the Practice of Garden Theory*. Philadelphia: University of Pennsylvania, 2000.

Ialongo, Ernest. *Filippo Tommaso Marinetti: The Artist and His Politics*. Fairleigh Dickinson University Press, 2015.

Kember, Sarah and Joanna Zylinska. *Life after New Media: Mediation as a Vital Process*. Cambridge, MA: MIT Press, 2012.

Kittler, Friedrich. *Gramophone, Film, Typewriter*. Stanford, California: Stanford University Press, 1999.

Kleinman, Adam 'Intra-actions' (Interview with Karen Barad)'. *Mousse* 34 (2012): 76–81.

Kurgan, Laura. *Close Up At A Distance: Mapping, Technology and Politics*. New York: Zone, 2013.

Lange, Susanne. *Bernd and Hilla Becher: Life and Work*. Translated by Jeremy Gaines. Cambridge, MA: MIT Press, 2007.

Lawrence Rainey et al., eds. *Futurism: An Anthology*. New Haven and London: Yale University Press, 2009.

Lepetit, Patrick. *Esoteric Secrets of Surrealism: Origins, Magic, and Secret Societies*. Rochester, VT: Inner Traditions, 2014.

Levi, Eliphas. *The Great Secret: Occultism Unveiled*. York Beach, ME: Samuel Weiser, 2000.

Ligotti, Thomas. *Teatro Grottesco*. London: Virgin, 2008.

———. *The Conspiracy Against the Human Race*. New York: Hippocampus Press, 2010.

Lovecraft, H.P. *Necronomicon: The Best Weird Tales of H.P. Lovecraft*. London: Gollancz, 2008.

Loyd, Anthony. 'McCullin's Last War'. *The Times Magazine* 29 December 2012: 8–19.

Lucic, Karen. *Charles Sheeler and the Cult of the Machine.* London: Reaktion Books, 1991.

Machen, Arthur. 'The Great God Pan'. In *Late Victorian Gothic Tales,* edited by Roger Luckhurst, 183–233. Oxford: Oxford University Press, 2005.

Marchand, Yves, and Romain Meffre. *The Ruins of Detroit.* Göttingen: Steidl, 2010.

Marder, Michael. *Plant-Thinking: A Philosophy of Vegetal Life.* New York: Columbia University Press, 2013.

Marinetti, Filippo Tommaso. *Critical Writings.* Edited by Günter Berghaus. New York: Farrar, Straus and Giroux, 2006.

Massumi, Brian. *Parables of the Virtual: Movement, Affect, Sensation.* Durham and London: Duke University Press, 2002.

McCarthy, Tom, Simon Critchley et al. *The Mattering of Matter: Documents from the Archive of the International Necronautical Society.* Berlin: Sternberg Press, 2012.

McCarthy, Tom. 'Science & Fiction, with a text by Tom McCarthy'. *The Photographers' Gallery Blog,* 15 June 2014. http://thephotographersgalleryblog.org.uk/2014/06/15/science-and-fiction-with-a-text-by-tom-mccarthy.

McCarthy, Tom. *C.* London: Jonathan Cape, 2010.

McCullin, Don. *Unreasonable Behaviour: An Autobiography.* London: Vintage, 2002.

McGrath, Laura. 'McCarthy, Marinetti and the Manifesto: New, Now and Never'. *Emerging Modernisms,* 17 August 2012. https://emergingmodernisms.wordpress.com/2012/08/17/mccarthy-marinetti-and-the-manifesto-new-now-and-never.

Merrin, William. 'Myspace and Legendary Psychasthenia'. *Media Studies 2.0,* 14 September 2007. http://mediastudies2pointo.blogspot.co.uk/2007/09/myspace-and-legendary-psychasthenia.html.

Miles, Barry. *William S. Burroughs: A Life.* London: Weidenfeld & Nicolson, 2014.

Milutis, Joe. *Ether: The Nothing That Connects Everything.* Minneapolis: University of Minnesota Press, 2006.

Mitchell, W.J.T., and Mark B.N. Hansen. *Critical Terms For Media Studies.* Chicago: University of Chicago Press, 2010.

Morris, Jacqui, dir. *McCullin*. British Film Company, 2012.

Nieland, Justus. 'Dirty Media: Tom McCarthy and the Afterlife of Modernism'. *Modern Fiction Studies* 58.3 (2012): 569–99.

Noyes Platt, Susan. 'Mysticism in the Machine Age: Jane Heap and The Little Review'. *Twenty One/Art and Culture* 1.1 (1989): 18–44.

O'Sullivan, Simon. *Art Encounters Deleuze and Guattari: Thought Beyond Representation*. Houndmills: Palgrave Macmillan, 2006.

Parry, Richard, dir. *Blood Trail: Shooting Robert King*. Revolver Entertainment, 2008.

Peirce, Charles Sanders. *Philosophical Writings of Peirce*. New York: Dover, 1955.

Penrose, Anthony. *The Lives of Lee Miller*. London: Thames and Hudson, 2013.

Penrose, Ronald. *Home Guard Manual of Camouflage*. London: George Routledge and Sons, 1941.

Pignarre, Philippe, and Isabelle Stengers. *Capitalist Sorcery: Breaking the Spell*. Translated by Andrew Goffey. Basingstoke: Palgrave Macmillan, 2011.

Poggi, Christine. *Inventing Futurism: The Art and Politics of Artificial Optimism*. Princeton: Princeton University Press, 2009.

Reynolds, Ann. *Robert Smithson: Learning from New Jersey and Elsewhere*. Cambridge, MA: MIT Press, 2003.

Shackleton, Ernest. South: *The Endurance Expedition to Antarctica*. Melbourne: Text Publishing, 1999.

Shimamura, Arthur P. 'Muybridge in Motion: Travels in Art, Psychology and Neurology'. *History of Photography* 26.4 (2002): 341–50.

Smajic, Srdjan. *Ghost-Seers, Detectives, and Spiritualists*. Cambridge: Cambridge University Press, 2013.

Smith, Daniel W. '"A Life of Pure Immanence": Deleuze's "Critique et Clinique" Project'. In Gilles de Deleuze, *Essays Critical and Clinical*, xi–liii. London: Verso, 1998.

Smithson, Robert. *The Collected Writings*. Edited by Jack Flam. Berkeley: University of California Press, 1996.

Solnit, Rebecca. *Motion Studies: Eadweard Muybridge and the Technological Wild West*. London: Bloomsbury, 2003.

Sontag, Susan. 'Godot Comes to Sarajevo'. *New York Review of Books,* 21 October 1993.

Stoehr, Taylor. 'Robert H. Collyer's Technology of the Soul'. In *Pseudo-Science and Society in 19th Century America,* edited by Arthur Wrobel, 21–45. Lexington: The University Press of Kentucky, 1987.

Thacker, Eugene. *Cosmic Pessimism.* Minneapolis: Univocal, 2015.

———. 'Dark Media'. In *Excommunication: Three Inquiries in Media and Mediation,* edited by Alexander Galloway, Eugene Thacker and McKenzie Wark, 77–149. Chicago: University of Chicago Press, 2014.

———. 'The Sight of a Mangled Corpse: An Interview with Eugene Thacker'. *Scapegoat: Architecture, Landscape, Political Economy* 5 (2013): 378–87. http://www.scapegoatjournal.org/docs/05/SG_Excess_378–387_F_Thacker.pdf.

———. *In the Dust of This Planet: Horror of Philosophy Vol. 1.* Winchester and Washington: Zero Books, 2011.

Uexküll, Jakob von. *A Foray into the Words of Animals and Humans: With a Theory of Meaning.* Minneapolis: University of Minnesota Press, 2010.

US Department of Defense. 'Embedment Manual'. In *Embedded: The Media at War in Iraq,* edited by Bill Katovsky and Timothy Carlson, 401–17. Guildford, CT: The Lyons Press, 2004.

Virgil, *The Aeneid.* London: Penguin, 2003.

Virilio, Paul, and Sylvère Lotringer. *Pure War.* New York: Semiotext(e), 1983.

Wark, McKenzie. 'The Drone of Minerva'. Public Seminar, 5 November 2014. http://www.publicseminar.org/2014/11/the-drone-of-minerva/#.Vci-1UWVJpl.

———. *Telesthesia: Communication, Culture and Class.* Cambridge: Polity, 2012.

———. *The Beach Beneath the Street: The Everyday Life and Glorious Times of the Situationist International.* London: Verso, 2011.

Wilson-Bareau, Juliet. 'Goya: Disasters of War'. In *Disasters of War: Callot Goya Dix,* 29–40. London: Cornerhouse Publications, 1998.

Zielinski, Siegfried. *Deep Time of the Media: Toward an Archaeology of Hearing and Seeing by Technical Means.* Cambridge, MA: MIT Press, 2006.

www.ingramcontent.com/pod-product-compliance
Lightning Source LLC
Chambersburg PA
CBHW072138170526
45158CB00004BA/1416